How to Raise a Girl

A Comprehensive and Actionable Guide to Help Your Daughter Along the Path to Adulthood

By reading this document, the reader agrees that under no circumstances is the author responsible for any losses, direct or indirect, which are incurred as a result of the use of information contained within this document, including, but not limited to, — errors, omissions, or inaccuracies.

"You haven't had the chance to choose the parents you have found, but you can choose which parent you want to be."

Marian Wright Edelman

Table of Contents

Introduction

Being a parent is not an easy job, which is why the last thing any parent would want is another set of rules on how to raise their kids. As overwhelming as bits and pieces of advice on parenting can be, they are still a necessity if we must raise our kids properly.

You need extra special care to raise a girl child, especially when she gets to puberty. Unfortunately, many parents and guardians—even moms—tend to shy away from teaching them what they need to know. One of the greatest mistakes a parent can make is to let their kids figure out for themselves vital information about their bodies and what is expected of them.

Every child is like a garden with seeds planted in it that can be nurtured into beautiful plants. Boys are like gardens with super-easy houseplants that require little of the gardener's attention. Think of the boy child like a garden of aloe plants— tough and durable. The girl child, on the other hand, is not simply a garden with any type of plants. Her garden is dotted with very delicate plants. Think of the girl child like a garden of maidenhair ferns or African violets—pretty but very fragile. Direct sunlight, too much water, too little water, over-touching, or the slightest change in soil acidity can damage these plants. The gardener (parent, guardian, or coach) has to take special care of these exquisitely fine but easily damaged plants. This is not to discount the efforts required to raise the boy child; nevertheless, the future of several generations depends on the upbringing of the girl child.

Different families have their unique values, as well as dos and don'ts that are peculiar to them. It is, therefore, nearly impossible to have one set of rules that will be suitable for every family with regard to how to raise their girl child. Irrespective of your personal views, the beliefs, family values, suggestions, and ideas presented in this book will help you effectively raise a daughter you will be proud of and who will be proud of the upbringing she received from her parents. The ideas presented in this book can be adapted to fit into your personal beliefs about how a child should be raised.

While this book will be an invaluable asset for mothers, every parent, guardian, teacher, and coach who seeks better ways to help raise a girl child will find this book very useful. Beyond the regular tips and pieces of advice for raising an all-around daughter, this book will also help the adult become a better parent.

Girls don't just turn out to be great daughters and women by accident. Someone has to invest time and effort into making sure that the "great daughter" outcome is guaranteed. I believe that someone should be you—her parent. I urge you to use the tools contained in this book to tend your garden. Prune it, weed it, and nurture it, and you'll be glad you did!

Chapter 1: A Note to Parents and Guardians

In the first few years of a child's stay on planet Earth, he or she gathers as much information needed to survive. The environment the child grows in is responsible for the information collected, and it will eventually shape the child's life. Parents and guardians have the greatest task of properly guiding the child to receive information that will program them for a future they will be proud of.

Most people grow up to discover that they do not like the life they are living. They go in search of ways to rewrite their inner programming to help them live the life they desire. Rewriting one's internal programming doesn't come easy; it takes time, sweat, and blood! It takes a lot of guts, sheer willpower, and an incredible ability to remain focused to change what has been built and programmed into the subconscious mind over several years. This is why a lot of people give up halfway into the journey and settle for less. This would not have been necessary if they were brought up in the right environment.

It is the responsibility of you as a parent or guardian to provide the right environment for the child. Nature made it such that parents come long before their offspring for a reason—to learn, test what they've learned by living it, adjust where necessary, and then teach their offspring to avoid the traps. This is the natural order of things.

So as a parent and guardian, your job is cut out for you already. Throwing your hands in the air in exasperation does not portray an image of one who has learned, tested, and adjusted well enough to care for a younger child. Your children are not beyond you. They are not too difficult— unless, of course, you have not fully understood what is required of you as a parent and guardian.

This book will remind you of what it is like to see the world from a child's perspective, especially the girl child. Once, you are able to take your mind back to how it feels like to be a child, you can easily speak the child's language, help the child see a little beyond their noses, and instill in them the correct information and value they need to become who they truly are.

Here are a few things to keep in mind as you seek ways to improve your parenting skills. The underlying message is pretty straightforward: you have to be a better parent for you to offer better parenting.

Give What You Have

"You cannot give what you do not have" is a cliché that almost every adult is aware of. Let me ask you: What are you giving the child under your care? What are your values? How well have those values served you? As a parent, aside from providing the basic necessities of life (food, clothing, shelter, and education), what else are you giving your child? Have you scrutinized the effects of what you are exposing your child to? Are you proud of your behaviors, and would you want your child to turn out like you?

For you to be able to raise a child properly, you first have the task of making sure that you have what it takes to raise a child. I am not referring only to your capacity to meet their physical needs; you also need to have the necessary mental and emotional tools to shape them into the image that they will be proud of.

You must begin to see yourself not just as a parent, guardian, or someone who is merely responsible for bringing another person into this world and giving them daily sustenance. You are a mentor! Begin to see yourself as a teacher who is saddled with the responsibility of fanning the flame that lies dormant inside the child. See yourself as a facilitator who brings out the best out of the child. See yourself as a mentor who has a mentee or a master who has an apprentice. Your goal is to bring the mentee or apprentice to maturity so that they will know what is right to do.

But how can you ever fill these shoes if you are deficient? How do you mentor your child when you are not equipped with the wisdom, knowledge, and capacity to do so? If the example of your life does not inspire greatness, how would mere words inspire your child to become great?

You need to embody what you want to give to your child. You need to become the living, breathing, and walking example of whatever training you want to give to your kids. Children, we all know, learn more by watching their parents and guardians. With kids, you cannot say one thing and do another and expect them to do what you say. They will settle for what they see you do, not what you say.

So, if you feel that you are lacking in some way, I suggest that you begin right now to take practical steps to improve your personal life. Read books (like what you're doing now). Attend workshops, seminars, and webinars, and so on. But do not put off raising your child until you have completely improved yourself. No. You will never get to a place where you will stop growing and improving. So, while you are making an effort to improve yourself, continue to positively influence your child with both your words and your actions.

Encourage Their Curiosity

You should not discourage the curiosity of a child; trying to do that will effectively squelch their creativity and affect their self-image.

One of the annoying questions you'll have to deal with is "Why?" Kids will ask you why the answer you gave them is that answer! They can drive you nuts with "Why?" Be patient. You were once like them—empty, innocent, and full of questions. The only way they can fill their minds with knowledge is to inquire about anything and everything. You are the be-all and end-all that they know, so you have to be ready to give them answers. If you don't, they'll get answers from other sources, which may not be reliable sources.

Don't Be Overprotective

"*I want my daughter to not make the mistakes I made*" is a good intention, but what answer will you give them when they ask why? Not why you don't want them to make the same mistakes but why you made those mistakes. If they do not understand why you made the mistakes you are frantically trying to stop them from repeating, they will always look for a way to find out for themselves. It is like blocking a water channel without opening another passage; water will always seek its level. It will create another path that you cannot stop.

Be there to offer guidance and protection, but do not deprive your children the opportunity to experience life for themselves.

Your Words and Actions Teach

Children are very impressionable; their minds are like an open blank page waiting to be written on. The thing is, they do not learn only by what they hear. In fact, they learn more by what they see you do than by what they hear you say. What this means is that you should be more deliberate and mindful of your words and actions, especially in the presence of your kids. One wrong move or one careless talk may create a completely wrong notion in your child.

Note to Dads

Isn't it funny to hear dads say they are babysitting their own child or children? "*Wifey is off to the salon,* so I'm *babysitting until she gets back.*" Really? Well, it's a common error, but dads don't babysit their own kids. To babysit means to look after or care for a child in the absence of the child's parents. You can look that up in your dictionary. You can only babysit a child that is not yours. If you are a legal guardian or a dad, then the time you spend with your child is called parenting, not babysitting.

Correct the perception that only moms are meant to take care of your kids. No. It takes two to make a baby, so the job of parenting involves both dads and moms. Dear dads, your job of parenting is not a temporal one. You are not filling in for the full-time parent (mom). You must see parenting as your primary responsibility and not a part-time thing you do in the absence of your wife.

Dads should not buy into the subtle message that says, "*You are too clueless to be a proper parent.*" It is both demeaning and a brazen display of sexism. Mothers are naturally equipped to provide for their children in ways fathers cannot (I mean, men don't breastfeed, do they?). But that does not mean in any way that dads cannot do all the other stuff that is involved in parenting. Surely, you are capable of offering encouragements, compliments, protection, and teachings. You can do all the other seemingly difficult tasks, like wiping butts, clearing vomits, bathing the kids, staying up late into the nights, and so on.

The point here is simple: The task of raising your child is a joint responsibility of both parents. Do not leave all for the mom.

Bottom Line

The job of raising children is not an easy one. You may not have signed up for it deliberately, but if you are a parent or guardian, your choices are limited. You'll have to step up your game and become more responsible, more responsive, and more reassuring. Your kids look up to you; don't let them down!

Chapter 2: Social Vulnerability

The girl child is beautiful! She's also more fragile and vulnerable to her environment than the boy child. From her physiology to her psychology, she is susceptible to external influences and can easily be swayed into thinking less of herself. To make sure that she doesn't grow up with that "*less than the opposite sex*" ideology, parents need to spend more time protecting and reassuring the girl child more than they do the male child.

While the boy child may feel embarrassed by too much show of affection by his parents, especially in public places (when he's with his peers), the girl child enjoys, expects, and welcomes such open display of attention and affection.

Boys are usually seen as strong and bold (even though not all of them are so), while girls are usually seen as weak, timid, and shy. Their hormones are responsible for making them feel and behave that way, so it is not their fault. Remember that nature is preparing the girl to become a future mother, and mothers are supposed to be tender, loving, and caring. Being abrasive is not a girly character, so do not expect your girl to be naturally bold, strong, and brave like most boys naturally tend to be.

Realize that your daughter deserves special tender care from you. See your daughter as having an invisible label on her forehead that reads: "Fragile: Handle with Care!" One of your responsibilities as a parent or guardian is to make the girl child understand that she is different from boys—not less than but different from boys—and that there is no reason to be ashamed of being different. Let her understand that she may appear weak in her physiology, but she is strong as can be.

Let us take a look at a few ways you can help your daughter weather the storm of social vulnerability.

Reassurance

Your daughter asks for reassurance from you in several forms. Sometimes she can ask you out of the blue, "*Am I beautiful?*" Don't just say yes and continue chatting away on your phone or watching TV. She needs to hear more than a simple yes. A simple yes does not convey the type of assurance she's seeking. Take your time to really appreciate her. Tell her all the positive things about her. She has to know why you feel proud of her.

Most times, your daughter will not be so direct or even use words. She may begin to try on makeup, put on a new dress, or just fidget with her hair. She is seeking attention. She wants someone who will speak positive words to her. Look out for these signs and cash in on that opportunity to make the bond between you and your daughter even stronger by inspiring a positive reaction in her.

We live in a world that is now more obsessed about image than ever. So, I'll suggest that you should be proactive as a parent and not wait for your daughter to ask directly or indirectly if she is beautiful before you tell her so. It is your responsibility to seize every opportunity you can to reassure her of how valuable you think she is both in her physical appearance and in her character, attitude, and personality. As a matter of fact, let your emphasis be more on her internal beauty than on her outward appearance.

There are three major ways you can communicate your daughter's beauty to her.

1. **By your words**: Your tone when you commend, praise, or say nice words to her matters a lot. The casual compliment doesn't work. You have to look her in the eyes and let her see that your words are from deep within you. Make her feel deserving and proud of herself by the glitter in your eyes. When you make statements such as "*You'll grow into a strong, intelligent, and fine lady,*" you are telling her that she deserves the best, and this will boost her self-confidence.

   Telling your daughter that she's beautiful is one thing; telling her that she makes her dress or whatever she's wearing beautiful is another level of compliment altogether. The message you should be aiming to pass across to her is that her beauty does not depend on what she wears; rather, she makes whatever she puts on beautiful. In other words, her beauty radiates all over her dress.

   When you do not say nice things about her looks, especially when she has gone all out to make herself look extra good, you leave her to wonder whether she is truly beautiful. Self-doubt begins to creep in, and she'll start to compare herself with other girls or the false beauty standards portrayed on the media.

2. **By your actions**: More than mere words, your actions carry a heavier salient message. Just as a picture is worth a thousand words, so do actions speak louder than words. Winking at your daughter, blowing her a kiss, or hugging her a few seconds longer will tell her more than any of your words can convey. Yes, she needs to hear you say, "*I love you,*" "*You are beautiful,*" "*You're a smart kid,*" and all the nice things; but all those things can be summed up in just one hug!

   Be spontaneous with your daughter, and this goes especially to the dads. Walk up to your daughter and ask her for a dance. Hold the door open for her to walk through while you're bowing to her. Do something—anything—that tells her, "*You are a princess and deserve more!*" You are in effect telling her that she is of value, and any responsible man would treat her that way too.

3. **By your reactions to other women**: This one is a bit tricky because it is not directed at your daughter. When you make demeaning statements about the looks of other women in the presence of your daughter, you plant a seed of doubt in her. She'll be left to wonder whether that's how you view her or view women in general, especially if it is a comment made by her dad. Girls are more self-aware of their physical features. When dads mindlessly throw words around in regard to a woman's feature, it can affect their daughter's self-image. For one, she may begin to wonder if she can ever measure up to the standard that men want. She looks up to her dad as the ultimate superman; whichever way her dad sees

women must be how women ought to be. Please do not give her a false standard that she'll never be able to live up to.

Encourage Assertiveness

Teach your daughter the difference between being rude and being assertive. Let her know that it is okay to be assertive without necessarily being rude. Encourage her to be polite but not shy. If someone is doing or saying something to her that she doesn't like, teach her to speak up. Tell her that standing her grounds with her peers doesn't mean that she is mean or will lose her friends. Let her know that it is not okay to cower in timidity just because she wants to be the good girl.

Teach her the difference between respect for adults and fear of adults. If she needs something, let her know that it is okay to express herself to an adult without being afraid.

Teach your daughter to know the difference between drawing unnecessary attention to herself and getting attention because she stands out as one of the best at what she does. Let her know that there is nothing wrong by being in the forefront, taking the lead, or being outspoken. And let her know, too, that it is okay if she doesn't like being outspoken. However, she should not let that be a basis for feeling less than others who are extroverts or thinking others are better than her.

Encourage her to engage in activities that are a natural fit for her, whether it is dancing, sports, or other extracurricular activities. The more exposed she is to these activities, the better and bolder she becomes.

Help Her Deal with Social Rejection

"*Everyone was invited except me!*" Now that could be really painful for your growing daughter. The way to help your daughter handle social rejection depends on her age.

For Preschoolers

If she's a toddler or a preschooler, she may think she's less than her peers, that's why she was left out. You will know by the sad and confused look in her eyes how she feels. In that case, explain to her that it wasn't meant to be an insult or to hurt her. Make her understand that sometimes we just get left out—it could be by mistake, or it could be that the other person just doesn't want us at their party or to play with them. Help your daughter to see that it is not her fault. It may have nothing to do with her but everything to do with her friend's mood.

However, before you jump into conclusion that your little daughter is feeling rejected or hurt, be sure that you are not causing more harm by intervening. For kids at that age, they may not be so aware of peer rejection. It may mean close to nothing to them when their friends don't want to play with them at the moment. Sooner or later, they'll get together again and play. But if you, as an adult, quickly step in to "save the day," you may be causing your daughter to wonder why you are making such a fuss about something so insignificant. Again, it may cause her to begin to think that there is something wrong with her and you are obviously trying to protect her from the kids who want to take advantage of her weakness.

While it may be heartbreaking for parents to see their kids turned down by their peers, do not make it into what it's not. Be sure that when you offer to help, you are not causing them more harm.

Also, it will be good if you observe your daughter's behavior as she plays with her peers. Take note of her preferences as she engages with other kids. What appears to be her difficulties with other kids? How well does she interact with small groups and large groups? What situations bring out the best in her? Use the answer to these questions to help her make friends.

For Teenagers

A teenager may think she's socially unfit or her friends simply want to insult her. The best way to help your teenage daughter through this type of psychological hurt is to help her reflect on the rejection.

Let her begin by considering her level of closeness with the person who rejected her. Was it someone she's had a long-standing relationship with or someone who is just an acquaintance or a friend of a friend?

She can then further reflect on why the rejection actually happened. Was it because of something wrong she did or was it purely out of malice? If it was something she did do wrong, this time of reflection gives her the opportunity to reconsider her actions and reactions in dealing with her peers. She'll have the opportunity to know what socially acceptable behaviors are and take necessary corrections. In such a case, encourage her to do the right thing and apologize for her wrong behavior. If the rejection has nothing to do with her, then she would have discovered firsthand what it means to have people around her who are not reliable. In such a case, encourage her to see that not all seemingly bad things happen to us because of something we did bad. Sometimes, people are just mean and try to take it out on beautiful young girls like her. It is their weakness and not her fault.

Reflection is a good thing to teach your teenage child because it helps her create a healthy mental state necessary for her overall well-being. When she learns how to reflect on situations, she'll not walk around with excess baggage of guilt, shame, and pain.

Help Her Avoid Bullying

Your daughter may be exposed to bullying. It is an unfortunate yet common occurrence, especially in schools or when an adult is not present. You need to teach your daughter to do the following:

- Stay away from places where bullying happens.

- Avoid bullies and avoid groups that are known for bullying.

- Stay close to an adult.

- Walk and eat in the company of friends when in school.

- Make new friends and always appear friendly.

- Never appear fearful. Walk and talk confidently without being arrogant.

Unfortunately, by the time most parents get to know that their child had been a victim of bullying, the incident must have occurred several times. This may not be your fault as a parent; it usually happens because your child is afraid of speaking up.

There are a number of things you could teach your daughter to do if she ever falls victim of bullying.

1. **Report to attack**: A lot of children find it difficult to talk to adults about the experience with a bully for a number of reasons. It could be that the child doesn't want to be seen as a weakling who can't stand for herself. It may also be that the bully threatened more attacks if she ever tells anyone.

   Encourage your daughter to speak up anytime someone threatens her and make her understand that you as well as other adults—like her counselor, teacher, and school nurse—are there to protect her. Tell her that the most responsible thing to do when someone is bullied is to report it to an adult. It doesn't make her a weakling or a snitch. It is simply the responsible thing to do.

2. **Be in control**: Usually, the first thing a bully is likely to do is to make sure they are in control of the situation in instilling fear in their victims. Once the victim cowers in fear, they take charge and inflict

bodily or emotional hurt. Teach your daughter to be confident or appear confident even if she's not. Being confident doesn't necessarily mean fighting back, arguing, or exchanging nasty words. It could simply be walking away confidently, standing her ground, or staring the bully down. If she learns not to give the bully control, she may discover that even though she was a bit scared, she could actually handle the situation.

3. **Change the mood**: Sometimes, a light comment or joke can disarm a bully. Teach your daughter ways to change the mood of a conversation by lightening the air. However, let her know the difference between making a light comment and making fun of the bully. One can make the bully back down; the other can infuriate the bully and make matters worse.

4. **Stand up for herself**: Teach your daughter to stand up for herself if she has accessed the situation and determined that it is safe to do so, or else, she should simply walk away. Teach her what to say or let her rehearse in front of a mirror. Teach her how to sound confident without coming off as cocky. Teach her that when she stands up for herself, she is helping others to become bold enough to defend themselves also.

5. **Don't fight back**: Discourage your daughter from fighting back. Fighting back may seem like the natural thing to do, but that could get her into more trouble. If the bully is hurting her physically, she should call for help and get away as fast as she can.

6. **Make new friends and get involved**: Encourage your daughter not to be a lone wolf in school. Let her

look for clubs, groups, and peers that share the same interest as her and hang out with them as often as possible. Make her understand that there is safety in numbers.

7. **Walk away**: One thing that is common with bullies is their need to be the center of attention; they want to be feared, not just by the person they are bullying but also by the small crowd that gathers. Advise your daughter to simply walk away when she is being bullied. Staying may cause other girls and peer group to gather around and intensify the humiliation. Calmly walking away even before the scene catches anyone's attention has a disarming effect on the bully.

8. **She shouldn't blame herself**: If there is anybody at fault, it is the bully, not the victim. The guilty party is the bully for behaving badly. Teach your daughter never to put the blame on herself for being attacked by a bully. Neither should she feel sorry for being unable to stand up to the attacker. Most times, the bully is physically stronger or commands more influence than the victim. So, her choice not to confront the bully was a wise one. She might not have been physically strong, but she definitely made the right choice by backing down.

Obviously, there is a need to teach your daughter how to access each situation and know which of the above methods to apply. Like Kenny Rogers, the musician, said, *"You've got to know when to hold 'em, know when to fold 'em, know when to walk away, know when to run."*

Reduce Exposure to Psychological Hurts

Compared to physical wounds, a psychological wound takes quite a long time to heal. In fact, they may last for a lifetime if they are kept afresh by mentally reliving the situations that caused it. This is why it is important to shield your child away from things that can trigger the reliving of psychological pain. This may not be 100 percent possible, but as much as lies in your power, reduce her exposure to things that remind her of a painful experience.

If a piece of music reminds her of a rejection she's recently faced, stop playing it. If your daughter shares a mutual friend with someone who had caused her pain, stop asking or talking about the mutual friend. If a certain route reminds her of the peers that jeered and humiliated her, stop taking her through that route. There are many situations, circumstances, events, and even people that will have to be removed temporarily or even permanently from her life if she must grow out of the psychological pain.

Differentiate between Verbal Abuse and Constructive Criticism

Teach your daughter, especially when she becomes a teenager, to ask clarifying questions that will help her differentiate between verbal abuse and constructive criticism. *"What exactly do you mean when you say that?"* *"Why did* you say that?" "In what way will that help me?" and suchlike questions are likely to reveal whether someone is offering constructive criticism or just verbal abuse. Make her understand that the underlying motive of constructive criticism is to help her. If you teach your daughter what constructive criticism is, she will be more open to receive it and also learn how to use it to correct her friends. On the other hand, make her see that verbal abuse is aimed at shaming, bullying, or mocking the individual. It may even present in the form of the silent treatment. If she is equipped with this knowledge, she can easily choose friends that will help her grow instead of those that aim to bully and put her down emotionally and psychologically.

Encourage her to never put up with bullying behavior just because she wants someone she can socialize with or because she craves company.

Help Her Improve Her Social Skills

While it may be true that some children are bullies who take undue pride in shaming other kids, it may be that your child is lacking in some of her social skills. If this is so, you will have to help her improve on her social skills to avoid reoccurrence of social rejection.

Teach her how to know when someone simply doesn't want to play, when someone is in a foul mood, when someone is just too busy to interact with her, or when someone is trying to end a conversation. If she doesn't know the cues to these things, she may find herself being rejected over and over again and begin to feel that there is something fundamentally wrong with her. Do not focus only on pointing out the times she is not behaving in a socially acceptable manner. Equally, remember to commend her when she's doing it right.

Again, teach her to be wary of sharing too much personal information with other people. Instead, she will be better off being a good listener.

Educate Her on Sexism

Unfortunately, there are still people who believe that there are some things that can be done only by boys and not girls. It is even reflected in some movies or TV shows. Do not allow these subtle messages to cripple your daughter's desire to do some things. Explain to her that, in the real world, things are completely different from what is obtainable on TV. Let her see that she can be, do, and have whatever she sets her mind to.

If she wants to play a particular type of sport, do not stop her. The fact that she is a girl does not mean she is limited to only certain types of sports. If she wants to participate in gymnastics or soccer, do not compel her to go for ballet classes. Allow her to figure out which sports she prefers. Being a girl doesn't mean she is a weakling! Avoid the temptation to assume what her strengths and weaknesses are. You may have read that girls are generally better than boys in reading tests and boys are generally better at math than girls, but that's just statistics. It has nothing to do with your daughter. So, allow her to run around in shorts playing soccer or let her go fishing if these things catch her fancy. Let her take things apart or figure out what makes things tick.

Allow her to play with the boys if that's what she wants. Do not assume anything; allow her strength and weaknesses to come to fore and then help her to work on improving the weaknesses while boosting her strengths.

Don't Be Too Quick to Offer Assistance

Give her the opportunity to prove her competence. Don't encourage her to believe she is the weaker sex. Even when she asks for help with her chores or homework, tell her to give it a little more try before you step in. Don't be in a hurry to offer her assistance at the slightest chance. Doing so will make her think she is truly a weakling and not good at performing tasks on her own. This will expose her to social attacks and ridicule, as she may not be able to be useful to herself amidst her peers.

Encourage Her to Be Her Authentic Self

Many parents seem to have a bias for kids that are extroverted. If you are not sensitive to your daughter's personality, you may unintentionally be forcing her to be who she's not. If she's introverted, allow her to be her authentic self. Do not compel her to become who she's not. If your daughter does not warm up quickly to strangers or prefers to be with smaller groups or even to spend time alone or with just one person at a time, do not act or make comments that suggest to her that she is odd.

If you want to see changes in her behavior, you will be more likely to succeed if you gently encourage the new behavior instead of trying to push your child or try to force a stop of the unwanted habit. Simply provide the opportunities that encourage new behavior. If you push your child when she is not ready or interested, you are putting her under undue pressure. If she is not ready to socialize in a way that you would prefer, please do not compel her.

Use Female Role Models

The world is brimming with female role models in every walk of life. Seize every opportunity you have to point out that fact. Pick out movies and books that have strong female characters for her to watch or read. Show her examples of female politicians, athletes, social workers, medical experts, authors, and so on. Above all, Mom is the first and best role model she can ever have. Remember in the opening chapter, I pointed out that you cannot give what you do not have. You cannot be a model to your daughter if you are lacking in good character. So, the work begins with you.

Chapter 3: Protecting the Girl Child

Generally, boys have no qualms doing certain things or taking certain decisions, like walking alone on a dark lonely street. However, girls are always aware of their physical vulnerability and always have a certain degree of fear or anxiety at the back of their minds. This is why your daughter needs constant reminders from you to make her feel safe and secured under your protection and shelter.

There are three broad ways your girl child will need your protection—emotional, physical, and spiritual protection.

Emotional Protection

Your girl can become doubtful of herself if she does not get a clear message from you that she is loved, she is beautiful, and she is priceless. A boy may consider constant assurances annoying, but a girl needs to hear and feel constantly reassured of her worth and value.

It is also important to keep an eye on her moods and behaviors. When you notice negative changes begin to show up, investigate. There is hardly any behavioral change that is unrelated to how she feels emotionally. Try to find out where the influence is coming from. What kinds of music does she listen to? What sites does she visit often online? Has she made any new friends that may be influencing her? You have to be observant to find out these things and take appropriate steps to remove the toxic source from her mind.

Physical Protection

There is an air of confidence your daughter carries around if she knows that you've got her back in no matter how ugly a situation gets. It can even show in her graceful steps and the way she talks! You boost her sense of security by being there for her no matter what.

This, however, does not mean you should encourage her to take undue risks. As a matter of fact, it is your responsibility to tell her about the possible dangers that are lurking in life's dark alley. Teach her how to stay safe and away from danger. Help her to know how to read in between the lines and to decipher danger from afar.

In making her see the dangers in the world, do not make her feel unsafe or paint a world full of scary monsters coming to get her. No. Your goal is to make her aware that not all that glitters is gold and that she should be wary of certain people, things, and events.

Sooner or later, your daughter is going to get hurt. That is a given. The important thing is to be there for her and to comfort her. Make her understand that being hurt is part of life and that we learn more by failing than we do by winning. She'll get hurt either by her making or for none of her own fault. If you scold her when she's hurting, you defeat the purpose for which she has you as her comforter. What she needs when she's hurting (even if it's her fault) is your comforting arms around her. She needs to know that "Mom and Dad are there for me even if the whole world turns against me."

Realize that growing up involves getting hurt in some way. She'll face failure, disappointments, and pain (both physically and emotionally). Do not deny her the opportunity of going through the experience of pain as long as it is not putting her life in any immediate or remote danger. Do not fuss over the small stuff. Allow her the opportunity to make age-appropriate decisions so that she can have firsthand experience of the consequences of her choices. This, of course, should be done within reason.

When you teach her how to stay safe, do not just stop at giving her some set of dos and don'ts. Remember to always look for opportunities to praise how smart she is in staying safe and out of trouble. And just in case she gets into trouble, as she most certainly will, be smart about rescuing her. Sometimes, girls, especially when they become teenagers, will prefer to take the risk of getting into trouble rather than face embarrassment in the presence of their peers and friends. So, you need to be smart about rescuing your daughter from such troubles.

Take the time to plan a series of SOS messages that are known only to the two of you. For example, she calls your phone and says something like, "*I'll be late. Please don't wait up for me.*" You immediately know she needs you to come and get her urgently. When she's in trouble and needs your help but doesn't want to appear fearful, she can send you the special SOS message, and you'll be there to rescue her.

Offering your daughter protection also means that you do not ignore the big stuff. Drugs and alcohol are not to be taken lightly. Be mindful if you begin to see empty cough syrup packages in her room or schoolbag. These days, prescription drugs are easily abused too. If you find your daughter indulging in drugs and alcohol, you must deal with the situation squarely. These things can mess with her mind and her ability to think clearly, which may put her in harm's way. Boys can take advantage of her by giving her alcohol or drugs. Let her know the consequences of these things.

However, it would be difficult to tell her not to engage in drugs and alcohol if you are neck-deep in the habit. Remember, you are her first role model.

Spiritual Protection

By spiritual protection, I do not mean praying for her, although that's not a bad idea. What I mean by spiritual protection is this: Guide her away from lies! Lies about what body shape she's supposed to have, how classy she's supposed to be, how "hot" she's supposed to appear, and all whatnots.

Protect her mind from the barrages of images and information flying freely. Your goal is not to prevent her from coming in contact with false information—you simply can't do that. Your goal is to instill in her correct information even before she begins to come in contact with the lies.

Your duty is to keep her constantly reminded of the fact that she is priceless and magnificent the way she is. Help her to look deep within her and follow her innermost excitement and bliss. Encourage her to cherish her uniqueness and fan the flame of her inherent talents.

Make your daughter see that her gifts and talents are deposited in her because she has a purpose in life. Make her understand that she's not on earth by accident. Teach her how to tap into her inner self and use her innate abilities for a purpose far much higher than mere selfish gains. Show her examples of great women who were once little girls or teenagers like her who went ahead a made great difference in the world. Make her see that she is no different from them. As a matter of fact, she can reach greater heights than they attained in their days.

The world is changing at a very rapid rate. Science and technology are continually rendering some jobs obsolete while creating fresh new jobs and career opportunities that never existed before. As a parent, it is your duty to help your daughter to identify careers that will remain relevant in the face of constant technological advancement. Make her see that traditional jobs are gradually being phased out and the future belongs to those who are prepared to think outside the box.

Give her the best education you can afford. And beyond academics, give her sound moral education too. Let your chitchats have lots and lots of inspirational messages so that she learns more each time she spends time with you. Remember when I said you must look at yourself as a mentor to your child? Well, this is one of the reasons. You shouldn't be drawing blanks when your daughter comes looking up to you for some piece of advice or suggestion. Do your homework well. Get yourself well equipped because that is the only way you can influence her life meaningfully.

Friends and peers groups are going to pressure her into several decisions. If she is not spiritually grounded, if she is not well educated at home, she can easily succumb to the pressures. But if she is properly informed, she'll seize the opportunity to also share her knowledge with her friends.

For Preschoolers

Your beautiful little girl appears so innocent; it is unthinkable that any human being in their right senses will want to hurt her. But not all human beings are in their right senses, so there is that tiny little chance that one crazy gunman can just open fire in public places for no just reason. Usually, little kids are unaware of such dangers, but when adults start to talk about it and they see it in TV stations, being analyzed and sending shivers down the spine of parents, little children will begin to take notice. They may not be in any immediate danger, but their innocent minds will be tainted by the fear of danger lurking in the dark.

Whether it is a gunman shooting sporadically in public places, like schools, or a rape incident that happened in another city, once your little girl catches wind of it, she'll need reassurance from you that she is 100 percent safe.

Talking to Your Preschooler about Violent Events

Here are ways you can help to calm your daughter and put to rest her fears.

1. First, you should find out what your daughter knows. You are an adult capable of abstract thinking and projecting current fears into future events. Your little daughter isn't good yet at such unfounded fears, so do not assume that she's afraid for her future as most adults are. What is on her mind is how that fear affects her in the present moment. Find out exactly how much information she has about the event that is causing fear and panic.

2. Be calm and let it pass if possible. Sometimes, it is not necessary to go into any lengthy explanation of why and how the event took place. Kids can easily forget their fears, especially if you are very calm about the issue. Your composure can dispel any fear they may have had earlier on.

3. Keep your explanations minimal and very simple. In the event that your daughter is eager to know what actually happened and what you think about it, simply give her the basics and leave out gruesome details. Let her have as much information that is healthy for her mind, considering her age, and stop at that. Do not give her information she has not asked for. And remember to use simple words that she can understand like "*bad man*" instead of "*gunman*" or "*crazy maniac*." Say "*hurt people*" instead of saying things like "*horrific*." Don't scare her more than she already is. Using harsh words to describe an already bad event is simply confirming her fears and making her to distrust her world.

4. Don't disregard her feelings. Although she may be just a kid, what she feels is very real to her. Please do not say, "*There's no need to be scared.*" Indeed, there is a need to be scared, and that's why she's scared!

Instead of disregarding her feelings, say something along the lines of *"I understand that you are troubled about what happened, but everything is going to be okay."*

5. Reassure her. She needs to hear you say, *"You are safe and protected and so is everyone you love."* Let her also know that her school is safe and protected. She'll take your word for it because at that age she trusts her daddy and mommy without a single doubt! Let her know that a lot of people are working to make sure that you all are safe.

6. Follow your usual routine. Unless there is an extreme and immediate danger, follow your usual routine. If you begin to overprotect your daughter or skip school or some other usual routines you observe, it will send her a signal that the situation is bad after all. So, go to the fun places you usually go, take a stroll around the neighborhood if that is your usual thing, or go for your usual fishing. The idea is to remain as calm as possible.

7. Keep her away from negative news. Mainstream media has a nasty habit of repeating news. If your daughter continues to see a replay of a horrible event on the news, she may think the event is happening all over again. Protect her innocence by keeping her away from news in all forms—TV, newspaper, and magazines. If you must discuss the event, make sure that she is nowhere nearby. And for heaven's sake, keep her mind occupied with things that have no bearing with the horrible event.

Bottom Line

In a world full of violent crimes against the female gender, protecting and sheltering your daughter should be top on your priority list. It goes without saying that your attitude about protecting your girl child should be "*Nothing is going to happen to you. Not on my watch!*"

Let your daughter know that she has a place where she can call home—a place where she is safe and secured from whatever is out there gunning for her, whether it is real or imaginary. If she has that knowing and assurance, she can confidently explore her world without the fear of being molested.

Chapter 4: Distorted Perceptions of Teen Girls

Perceptions shape our realities, whether we are adults, kids, or teens. If you notice toxic behavior in your teen girl child, it is very likely that she's picked up some thwarted perception somewhere, and it is up to you to help her correct that perception. Most of the time, these perceptions, which show up in the form of toxic behaviors, are a reflection of deep-seated fear.

Care must be taken to address these fears and not just the symptoms (behaviors) of the fears. Create a conducive atmosphere that encourages your daughter to open up to you to share her deepest fears. You can do this by sharing your own fears, too, and how you overcame them. Show her how your fear tainted your perception and how dealing with the fear cleared up your outlook about life.

In the teen years, girls are very susceptible to external influences that can dramatically affect their views of life. I'll share some of these distorted views that have many teenage girls trapped in the prison of their own unfounded fears. When you notice any of these false premises in your daughter, you will do well to help her shift her perspective.

Life Is Boring without Gadgets

True, laptops, phones, and tablets really make life easy; but they are not a requirement for living a truly happy and fulfilled life—not for adults and definitely not for kids.

Let your daughter understand that the pursuit of her dreams is more important and adds more value to her life than wasting away on social media. You can help her see how more productive she is when she's not focused on her gadgets by creating practical experiments for her.

Tell her to do this:

1. Get her a notebook and label it "My Special Productivity Notebook."

2. Let her spend one whole week focused on her studies, chores, time with friends, and time with siblings and family.

3. Every night for that one week, just before she goes to bed, let her write down the number of things she was able to accomplish in her special productivity notebook.

4. At the end of whatever accomplishments she's written, let her mentally gauge her happiness level and write it down on a scale of 0 to 10—0 being absolutely pissed, angry, or sad and 10 being a state of utter bliss and happiness.

5. At the end of the first seven days, let her begin another round of seven days. This time, let her use her gadgets as much as she wants without caring

whether she has completed her homework or chores.

6. Every night for the second week, she should write down the number of things she was able to accomplish in her special productivity notebook.

7. She should also write down her happiness level before she sleeps.

8. At the end of the second week, she should compare her productivity level between week 1 and week 2. It will be glaring to her that her happiness does not depend on gadgets; neither does too much attention to gadgets improve her productivity level.

I Must Be Mean to Be Respected

Cliques can be very influential in the life of young girls. There seems to be some sort of unwritten code among teen girls that says, *"We have to be the meanest gang so that others won't dare mess with us!"*

If you think boys are bullies, wait until you see what girls are capable of. Mean girls can do the following:

*   Rip each other apart with insults.

*   Use body shaming and say mean things and very nasty remarks to create self-doubt in their fellow teenage girls.

*   Employ the silent treatment or passive aggression to make another girl feel completely unwanted.

- Deliberately leave someone out.

- Use backstabbing, rumors, and gossips as a deadly weapon to run down another girl's reputation.

- Leak personal information or someone's secret to cause hurt and embarrassment.

Boys can cause physical hurt when they bully; they hurt you from the outside. When you see a boy who bullies, his appearance tells you he's a bully. But girls who bully mostly do it from within. Physical hurt can easily pass, but inner pain lasts much longer. Plus, girls look so sweet and innocent that even adults will have a hard time believing your story when you make a report. They will smile and hug you but spread nasty rumors behind your back.

Girls literally take bullying of other girls to another level entirely. But don't get me wrong. This is not to say all girls are involved in this appalling habit. In fact, those who do may have been forced into it by the ringleader of the clique so that they will also avoid being bullied. However, the need to identify with one mean clique or the other so as to avoid being bullied is absolutely backward. Refer to chapter 2, where I listed a couple of ways you can successfully help your daughter to avoid bullying.

This type of behavior stems from a fear of being rejected. To suppress that fear, girls lash out by being mean and then join others who are also mean because there is strength in numbers.

You need to teach your girl that there is no need to be in competition with anyone in school, at home, or anywhere. Teach her that there is a virtue in being a good and kind person. Show her that being a mean person only leaves her hurt, angry, and depressed. Teach her that true respect cannot come from causing her peers pain and fear. Make her understand that true respect only comes from a deep sense of self-respect and a genuine desire to be of help to others. Encourage your teenage daughter to find friends who motivate and inspire her to see the good in others and to avoid peers who are preoccupied with tearing others down.

I Need Approval from Others

Every teenage girl wants to know that she's accepted and can go to any length to get that approval unless she is guided properly. The need for approval and attention comes from a twisted belief that her self-worth depends on how others see her. So, she goes all out to meet the expectation of others, especially her friends and sometimes boys. Other times, some teenage girls would want to prove themselves to their coaches, teachers, and parents.

The kinds of thoughts that occupy their minds when they are feeling less than others may go like this:

- "Nobody wants me because I'm not good enough."

- "I'm worthless. Even boys don't look my way."

- "If only I can get a boyfriend, others will approve of me."

- "I don't have close friends because I'm stupid."

- "I'll never be good enough unless I meet certain standards."

- "If I can get the approval or attention of this person, then I'll feel complete."

They think this way because they seek external validation of being accepted. This is why an adult needs to guide them to seek validation from within themselves. If this guidance is not available, your teenage girl may run herself in a state of desperation and begin to engage in all sort of things just to prove that she is worthy of attention and approval. This may include the following:

- Giving in to peer pressure

- Resorting to the use of drugs and alcohol

- Brushing aside moral values received from home

- Engaging in sex to prove that she is also capable of being like others

Parents, guardians, teachers, and coaches need to be proactive to ensure that young girls understand that their self-worth does not depend on being accepted by other people. It is important to teach teenage girls to always keep their focus on the positive aspects of their lives—to concentrate on the things they like doing whether others are interested in them or not. Teach them that they are unique and must not throw away their uniqueness simply because they want to blend with every other person or to follow a trend. Encourage them to be proud of who they are and what they love to do even if their peers or boys don't seem interested in them.

This can be a very challenging concept for teenage girls to grasp as no one likes to be the odd one out. But make them see that it is okay to stand out as unique. Show them the value in being different. Let them know that the right set of friends will be drawn to them if they do not let down their standards in order to live up to the expectation of others.

If there is one important message you need to drum into your daughter, it is this one: *To bring quality people into her life, she should stand her ground and uncompromisingly own who she is. It makes her develop a thick skin against rejection and gain all the respect she rightfully deserves.*

Thankfully, these types of distorted beliefs can be noticed in young girls before it grows into a full-blown self-limiting belief. Watch out for these signs:

- Going out of her way to please another person

- Taking extra time doing her makeup

- Feeling constantly depressed and moody

- Condoning being bullied just to keep a friendship

When you notice any of these signs, it is possible that your sweet teenage daughter is having issues with her sense of self-worth or some other twisted perspective about herself and the world around her. Gently step in and help her out.

I Am Ruined

If you do not take steps to help your daughter out of low self-esteem, she can go to lengths that may hurt her physically or emotionally. If this occurs, she'll be left with a feeling that says, "*I am ruined!*" For example, a girl who seeks external attention and validation and rushes into engaging in sexual activities may end up with a heartbreak that leaves her devastated and an emotional wreck. "*He used me!*" continues to linger in her head. She'll begin to see herself as a failure. She's failed her parents and herself because she was so stupid to give in to peer pressure. And because she is immature to process these emotional ups and downs, she may end up suppressing these feelings and suddenly become aloof. Your sweet teen girl now goes about with excess baggage of guilt and shame. She's bought into a lie that says she deserves to be punished because she has failed. She'll begin to dissociate herself from things or people that make her feel loved because she feels she doesn't deserve to be loved. "*I am bad, and bad people are unworthy of love.*" In some girls, instead of feeling guilt and shame, and becoming detached, they lash out and become rebellious.

You can nip all this in the bud by having regular chats with your daughter. Encourage her to share with you her deepest worries and fears. Even when she's not forthcoming, you can persuade her gently. Show her that you have fears and worries too. Ask her opinion about what you should do to wriggle out of your worries and fears. When she sees how open you are with her, she'll take the cue and gradually open up to you.

I Need to Have the Ideal Body Type

The earlier you teach your teenage daughter that there is no ideal body type, the sooner she'll get over obsessing about the perfect body type. Always remind your daughter that her body is beautiful the way it is. It doesn't matter if she has stretch marks, curves, no curves, muscles, six-pack abs, small boobs, or large boobs. What really matters is that she is comfortable in her own skin. Encourage her to always focus on what her body can do instead of obsessing unnecessarily on what her body should or should not look like.

You can help her by showing her female role models with different body types and shapes. Make her understand that the container (her body) doesn't matter as much as its contents.

I Need a Boyfriend to Be Happy and Socially Acceptable

The quest to fit in and be accepted among her peers can make your teenage girl think that girls without boyfriends are not cool. This is a lie that many teenage girls find themselves believing, and it can lead to a host of other lies and heartbreaks.

As parents and guardians, your role here is a very delicate one. You must find a balance between protecting her from being gullible and letting her make a choice of her own. The truth is that parents will always think their daughters are still kids when it comes to relationship issues, but sooner or later, these teenagers will have to experiment for themselves with or without the parents' approval.

There is actually nothing wrong with girls wanting to have boyfriends; however, make it clear to your daughter that her desire to go into an intimate relationship should be because she actually finds someone she cares about and not because she has to do it to be socially acceptable.

Make your daughter understand that relationships are not entered because it's a cool thing to do. No. It's not about being cool or about following a trend. It is about mutual respect, trust, and finding someone who brings out the best in her. Also, help your teenage daughter see that her happiness does not depend on anyone outside of herself, not even a boyfriend!

Explain to your daughter that relationships do not always go as planned. Her heart could be broken into a thousand pieces, she may lose her self-control and have sex, she may be forced into sex, she may contract STDs, and so on. But be balanced in your presentation of the facts and let her know, too, that she may be in for a lifetime of fun love and a dedicated relationship. As much as you would like her to be safe, allow her to make her own mistakes as long as they are not life-threatening or life-altering mistakes.

Above all, let her see that she doesn't have to say yes to the first boy who approaches her or chase after the first boy she thinks about. There are many boys that will come her way, and she has a whole lifetime to make a good choice. Teach her that there is absolutely no need to rush into having a boyfriend as a teenager if she really doesn't want it.

I Am Now an Adult and Can Do as I Please

Adolescence is not the same as adulthood, but teenagers don't seem to know that distinction. At first, puberty gets them all confused. They think they have it all figured out. *"I'm growing boobs like Mom. I must be an adult!"* And they go all out to act like the adults they see around. Here lies the rub: if you have not been a good example up until now, it is difficult to expect your teenage girl to act like a responsible adult all of a sudden. If you've not always been around for her to emulate good characters from you, then she'll pick up habits from the next best option—the TV, internet, or even magazines.

Help your teenage daughter understand that her physical features and hormones may make her think and feel she's an adult, but adulthood comes with a whole lot of responsibilities that she's not yet capable of bearing. Teach her to take it one step at a time; after all, she has an entire life to be an adult.

"You're my daughter! You're my responsibility as long as you're still living in my house!" That's a poor way to make her understand responsible behavior. If anything, you are pushing her to think, *"Well, I guess I'm going to look for my own house or someplace where I wouldn't be treated like a child!"* For heaven's sake, teaching, encouraging, and guiding your teenager doesn't need to come to quarrels and shouting matches. That's like switching roles. She's acting like an irresponsible adult, and you are acting like an unreasonable child!

Realize that dealing with your girl as a teenager requires the use of kid gloves. Kids don't need kid gloves as much as teenagers do! You can tell a girl child no, and she will simply understand. Not a teenage girl! You'll need more than just a "no" to make her understand.

Your job as a parent becomes tougher when your daughter becomes an adolescent. The earlier you realize this, the easier it will be to understand her point of view. If you confront, oppose, and push her at this stage of her life, she may veer off into a downward spiral. Your approach should be gentle and tactful.

I Need to Be Sexually Active to Be Cool

Teach your daughter that there is nothing wrong with staying away from sexual activity until she is matured enough to handle it. While it is true that society has made people believe that no girl saves her virginity until she gets married, having sex at an early age doesn't make a girl cool or not cool.

It is your duty as a parent to be unbiased in your presentation of the facts. Teach her that having strong moral values is the coolest thing ever because it will make her self-esteem shoot sky-high! Make your daughter see that there are lots of kids who do not engage in smoking, drugs, or alcohol yet are really cool kids. The same goes for being sexually active; she doesn't have to engage in it to be the coolest kid on the block.

To help her maintain her sense of moral values, encourage her to make friends with peers that are groomed with the same set of moral value.

Parents Are So "Yesterday"

If your daughter thinks you are old-fashioned, out of touch with current trends, or just plain stupid, it may not be entirely her fault; and neither is it any of yours. The way parents are portrayed in many TV shows and movies may have influenced that notion.

You do not have to compete with your kids in this regard to prove that you are also "cool." Instead, do the following:

- Teach them that human perceptions and development needs to be on a continuous forward movement in order for any meaningful advancement to take place.

- Make them understand that you are there to guide them from falling into potholes along the path of life's journey but that obviously things cannot remain the way they used to be when you were younger.

- Make it a point of duty to share ideas with them and compare notes from time to time. If you engage in this, you'll learn new stuff that'll make you a "cool mom" or "cool dad." This will also show them where there may be potential danger or error in their points of view.

The point is, you should be ready for mutual learning instead of imposing your "old school" ideas on the new generation.

Bottom Line

As your daughter grows into a beautiful teenager, she becomes more aware of her surroundings and tries to blend in with her environment. Because of her somewhat naive nature, she can be easily swayed into believing all types of falsehood disguised as "acceptable social practice" by peers who are misguided or from ideas and opinions presented on TV, in magazines, and on the internet.

It is your job as a parent or guardian to hold high the compass of what is right and wrong to help her navigate the myriad of turbulent perceptions. Remember that she is not yet an adult; she's on her way there. The day you helped co-create her (or adopt her into your home), you also signed up to provide her with proper guidance until she becomes capable of navigating life by herself.

Chapter 5: Personal Hygiene

It is important to start reinforcing the need for personal hygiene from an early age. Doing so will help your child get used to the idea of taking good care of herself even before she gets to puberty.

Every child learns in different ways. You will have to know what method your child prefers—demonstrating so that she emulates, showing her what to do, or telling her verbally. Your child needs your support at this age to remain clean and healthy and to learn and imbibe proper hygiene.

Here are a few ways to encourage your child to get used to taking care of her body and her personal hygiene:

1. Shower her with lots of praises when she carries out any hygienic activity.

2. Constantly remind her to take a bath or shower, floss, wash, and keep her hands clean. If she's a pre-teen or a teenager, remind her to use deodorants, body sprays, or perfumes and to shave. Before long, she'll get used to the idea.

3. Break the hygienic tasks into smaller steps, like a written schedule or a to-do list with a specific time attached to each task. After following this routine for a while, she will automatically remember to perform

the tasks at the right time.

4. If she's already a teenager, allowing her to pick her
    deodorant, antiperspirant, perfume, toothpaste,
    tampons or pad, and underwear will equally
    encourage her to remember to use these things as
    well as to keep herself clean.

The perfect time to start to teach your daughter personal
hygiene is when she's just a toddler. Of course, you'll have to
do everything for her, but she'll get the idea quickly as she
grows older. So, reminding her of things like bathing
regularly or bathing after sweating profusely (like after
exercising), not picking her nose, not picking scabs, and
washing her hands each time she uses the toilet will help her
become a better adolescent.

While you may simply make your little preschooler do what
you want her to do, pre-teens and teenagers will need extra
reminders to take care of themselves. As your daughter starts
to approach puberty, the changes in her don't just make her
grow into an adult; they also make her body start to require
special attention. If she doesn't know how to give her body
this special attention, she may not look, feel, and smell as
nice as she used to when she was only a little bundle of joy.

Body odor, vaginal discharges, menstrual periods, sweats,
hair, and bacteria in the armpit and so on all mean one
thing—more cleanliness. She needs to know how to remain
clean always so that she'll grow into a beautiful young
woman.

Body Odor

Kids smell nice naturally, but as they begin to approach puberty, their bodies begin to secrete hormones that cause funny smells and make them stink. It happens to every child at puberty. Increase in the rate of perspiration as they mature can also cause them to smell funny. Discharges from the vagina can also leave some odd smells lingering on her body.

Here are a few ways to make sure she keeps body odor away.

1. Encourage and remind her to take regular baths even when she doesn't feel like it. Preteens and teenagers can be naughty at times; they can be out of the bathroom in less than two minutes! So, you need to ensure that she takes her bath properly. Emphasize the need to always wash her armpit, private part, and feet to avoid odd smells.

2. Buy her a nice deodorant. Antiperspirants can also help to reduce body odor, but check to make sure you are giving her a product that is safe for her skin.

3. Teach her how to use perfume moderately. Drenching herself in perfume in a bid to smell nice is counterproductive. She can spray twice or thrice into the space in front of her and then walk through the spray.

4. Facial hair and hair on her arms and legs are not unhygienic. After all, boys and men have and keep them, yet a lot of them are very neat and hygienic. Teach your daughter to shave her arms and legs if she likes to. It is purely a matter of choice.

5. If she chooses to shave any part of her body, let her know that it is better to use shaving soap or cream to avoid skin irritation, bumps, and nicks.

6. To avoid smelly feet, teach her to properly dry her feet after bath before putting on her shoes. It doesn't matter whether she is sporty or not. If her feet are damp inside her shoes for a long time, it will cause them to become smelly.

Private Part

1. Teach her how to wash her private part when bathing. No soap or abrasive agent should be used. Water is all she needs.

2. Help her to keep her private part clean, dry, and well ventilated by wearing loose-fitting underwear and breathable fabrics. Polyester clothing may reduce ventilation and increase her moisture and temperature levels.

3. Teach her how to shave her pubic hair and the hair under her armpits. Moms can be practical about this. For dads (especially single dads), this could be a bit tricky. I'll suggest you stick with verbal explanations alone. Single dads (and moms too) can show her magazines or video clips that can help guide her.

Tampons and Pads

When she eventually begins to menstruate, you'll have to help her decide whether to use a tampon or a pad. Both are excellent choices with different advantages. But more than their advantages, she'll need to know how to care for her private part and how to use these things.

Dear Mom, please do not shy away from this responsibility. You are raising another potential mother. If she doesn't learn these things from you, she probably won't be able to teach her own daughter and other girls too. No girl is born with this knowledge; they have to learn it from someone. In my opinion, there's no better person to do the teaching than you!

Here are the basics she needs to know:

Tampons

- Help her to choose her tampons if you both have chosen to use it instead of a pad. There is no need to select a tampon that comes with deodorants. It may cause irritation to her vagina.

- Tampons are inserted into the vagina to trap the blood before it flows out.

- They are very convenient to use, but she can easily forget to change them since they are not visible. Set reminders on her cell phone to prompt her to change them at intervals.

- Remind her that it is very necessary to change tampons every four to six hours. It can cause bacterial infections and odor if left inserted for longer periods.

- Leaving the tampons in for longer periods may cause blood to leak unto her underwear.

- Teach her never to put a tampon in throughout the night or all day. Doing so may cause a rare but dangerous disease known as TSS (toxic shock syndrome).

- Teach her never to flush used tampons (even if the box says she can). Wrap it in a toilet paper and trash it.

- If she's concerned about swimming during her menstrual period, she definitely should use a tampon. Plus, it can be worn with any outfit—bikini bottoms, skirts, and shorts—because it is not visible.

Pads

- Teach her how to attach a pad to the inside of her underwear. A practical demonstration or verbal instruction will do the job.

- Tell her the possible dangers of using scented pads or those with deodorants. They can cause irritation or allergic reactions.

- She needs to know that pads should be changed every three to four hours. This will help to prevent a buildup of harmful bacteria as well as reduce the chances of producing odor.

- If she has a heavy menstrual flow, help her to choose pads that are designed for heavy flow. Remind her that she has to change frequently to prevent leakage that can occur because of oversaturation.

- If your daughter likes to swim, let her know that she cannot use a pad during her menses if she intends to swim. In that case, a tampon is a better choice.

- As with tampons, instruct her never to flush a used pad. To dispose of used pads, teach her to carefully wrap them in a toilet paper and throw into a trashcan.

Underwear and Bras

1. Teach her to wash her underwear frequently.

2. Provide her with a fair collection of underwear. It is a good practice to not repeat the same underwear twice in a row without washing. Let her always have clean spare underwear in her school bag so that she can change as soon as she notices there is some sort of discharge on the one she is wearing.

3. When buying her underwear, encourage her to select cotton underwear that is comfortable.

4. Please do not encourage her to use G-strings.

5. Make it abundantly clear to her that under no circumstances should she wear someone else's underwear. She runs a high risk of getting infections.

6. When her breasts begin to bud, it is good to get her a bra. You can help her to select a bralette, training bra, or a sports bra since she's still in the early stage of developing her breasts. The goal is to provide modesty and some form of support while the breasts are still developing.

7. Picking a bra for your teenage girl can be an exciting moment for her or not. But in any case, she'll get used to it. The fact is, beyond buying colorful and stylish bras, teach her how to keep them clean always through frequent washing.

8. Help her understand that a sweaty bra is not good for her breasts and skin. If she's going to be engaged in sporting activities in school, it is advisable to have a spare bra in her school bag to change immediately after sports.

9. Tell her to give her breasts some breathing space! It is okay to sleep in a bra if that's what makes her comfortable, but being on bra 24/7 isn't ideal either.

There is no specific age at which every girl must start using a bra. Girls are different, and so is their breast development. However, any of the following situations is a cue that your girl needs a bra.

- When her breasts start to bud (this is a no-brainer)

- When your daughter asks to shop for a bra

- When all or most of her girlfriends wear one

- When she's engaged in sporting activities and needs extra support for her breasts

- When there is a need for extra cover because her breasts are beginning to become noticeable through her clothing or when she starts becoming uncomfortable not wearing one

- When your teenage daughter is going for sleepovers or there'll be a need for her to change her clothes in school

Hair, Face, Oral, Nails, and Clothing

- Let her know that it is not necessary to wash her hair on a daily basis. Washing her hair daily can quickly deplete the natural oils in her hair and scalp. These oils are needed to keep her hair hydrated.

- Help her to select shampoos and conditioners that suit her hair type. Teach her how to properly wash and rinse off shampoo and conditioner from her hair.

- Wearing dirty clothes will make her look unkempt. She has to learn how to wash her clothes and wear neat clothes, or else it will defeat the purpose of having a hygienic body.

- Encourage her to always wash off makeup before going to bed. Using mild soap and water is perfectly okay to keep her face clean and healthy. The use of face cleansers and moisturizers are equally great but completely optional.

- Encourage her to always keep her fingers and toenails trim to prevent dirt and possible germs. Some kids are used to biting their nails; this is a bad habit. Ensure to discourage it very early before it turns into a habit.

- If she desires to paint her nails, let her know that it is okay to do so as long as she doesn't do it too frequently. Using nail polish too frequently can cause her nails to become weak and yellowish. This may not be unhygienic, but it is rather unsightly.

- Ensure that your child brushes twice daily and floss regularly.

- It is important to keep the mouth always clean and keep regular appointments with the dentist to avoid tooth decay, bad breath, and gum problems.

Food and Drinks

- Teach your daughter the importance of staying hydrated always. She can even carry a bottle of clean water in her bag to make sure she stays well hydrated. It will help to improve the look of her skin.

- While it is good to stay fit and eat healthy, explain to her that it is very unhealthy to starve herself just because she wants to be slim and fit. Teach her that being skinny isn't better than being who she is. She can eat several smaller meals instead of avoiding food.

- Advise her on the need to eat healthily and avoid junk foods. On your part, ensure that the meals you provide are balanced and healthy.

- Explain to her the dangers of getting drunk. Let her see that alcohol is not good for her health. It is also capable of making her make the wrong choices or bad decisions.

Physical Fitness

Obesity has been identified as the most prevalent nutritional disorders among young children in the United States (The Journal of Clinical Endocrinology & Metabolism, 2018). One study revealed that "There is no indication that the prevalence of obesity among adults and overweight among children is decreasing. The high levels of overweight among children and obesity among adults remain a major public health concern" (US National Library of Medicine, 2004).

Given the above facts, it is very important for parents to take steps early enough during the child's development to prevent overweight. However, be careful not to simply assume that your child is becoming overweight and then begin to make drastic changes to her diet. Growth in children is not easily predictable because each child has their own unique growth pattern based on their body structure. This is why the best approach is to get a health-care professional to determine whether or not your child is putting on excessive weight for her age.

Here are some quick tips to help you prevent childhood obesity.

1. Be an example of healthy eating and physical activity without necessarily focusing on a particular weight goal.

2. Encourage your family to eat together as often as it is feasible. This will help you monitor to some extent what your child eats.

3. Set and maintain daily eating times as well as when it is okay to have snack.

4. Serve age-appropriate portions of food to avoid overeating.

5. Provide a variety of healthy foods.

6. Discourage sedentary habits. Allow your child to have adequate time for play, especially those involving physical activity.

Bottom Line

Aside from keeping your child in good health, good personal hygiene will help boost your daughter's self-esteem and confidence level. She will be comfortable to interact freely with other people if she smells nice, looks nice, and has nice breath too. The reverse is true if she's unkempt and smells funny. It can also affect her self-image negatively.

If it seems like there are too many things to remember or to teach, simply lead by your good example. For moms, all you need to do is simply tell your daughter to emulate you. You are an adult and have already done most of these things many times, so they will come naturally to you. You only need to remember to tell her to do what she sees you do and explain to her why it is necessary to do these things. For dads, you will probably feel embarrassed about dealing with certain topics or you don't know how to do it properly, but strive and remember that all this is extremely natural and concerns the well-being of your beloved daughter.

Chapter 6: For Single Dads

Children observe their environment not passively but actively. They try to classify the behaviors of their first teachers—their parents—into categories of the male and female gender. A boy child who grows with both parents is likely to think that every behavior of his father is strictly for males, and a girl who grows with both parents may likely think that all her mother's behaviors are strictly for females. For example, a little boy who observed that his dad always brushes with a blue toothbrush and his mom uses a yellow toothbrush may conclude that blue toothbrushes are for the male gender while yellow toothbrushes are for females. Imagine how surprised the boy will be the first time he sees a man brushing his teeth with a yellow toothbrush!

As children grow older, this type of thinking is soon replaced with correct thinking because they will begin to see more clearly that their parents' behaviors are not necessarily tied to their gender.

The point is that single dads must be ready to model both roles of mom and dad for their little daughter. Raising a child as a single parent isn't easy, but the load is a bit lighter if a dad is raising a boy child. For single dads who are saddled with the responsibility of raising a daughter, this task won't be a walk in the park.

You may be a dad who is widowed, divorced, separated, or unmarried with a daughter; the challenges of raising a girl child is the same for these circumstances. I have listed below a few tips that can be of immense help for single dads who must raise beautiful, strong, responsible, and confident daughters.

Enlist the Help of a Female Mentor

No matter how well you try to play the role of a mother, your daughter still needs a female figure—someone who has the same physiology as her—to look up to. An adult female's perspective is very important for your daughter so that she can gain a balanced view of life. There are several women who can fill in this position in the absence of the mother (living or late).

- An aunt or her grandmother

- Your sister, especially if she has a girl child who is your daughter's age or if she has older girls

- A trusted female friend

- A trusted female church member

- A female athlete coach or a female girl scout leader.

The bottom line is that she needs a female figure to model after. Don't deny her that opportunity.

Listen to Her

The way a lot of men are wired is to have this attitude of fixing things. But sometimes, your daughter doesn't need you to fix her issues. She just needs someone who would actively listen to her for the sole purpose of understanding her and being empathetic. When your daughter speaks with you, listen and connect with her. Showing that you feel what she's feeling is more important to her than listening half-heartedly only to run along, looking for how to make her problems go away. You girl child wants to learn through communication rather than through doing.

Coach Her to Solve Problems

To raise a confident girl, you need to coach her to be a problem solver. Don't rush in every time to help her solve problems. Coach her to develop the skills required to think through problems, breaking them down into simple, doable steps and actually taking those simple steps to solve the problems. Do not make your daughter rely 100 percent on you for every little problem she encounters.

Equally, it is important to make her understand that life isn't about all or nothing. Show her that if she fails at one thing, she should have other backup plans to fall back on. Teach her that life is choosing between several options and not just choosing between making it or failing. That way, she will approach each problem with several alternative solutions instead of giving up as soon as her only solution doesn't work.

Let Her Try Things Out Herself

To further build her self-confidence, expose her to some degree of risks. So long as that challenge will not cause her any harm, let go of the need to rescue her from it. Allow her to use her intuition and the things you have taught her. What would be the point of teaching her how to be a problem solver if you do not give her the opportunity to solve problems? This is a rather difficult aspect of parenting, especially for dads who have only one child and she is a daughter. How to let go of complete control is a daunting challenge for dads. They almost always envision that the world out there will come crashing on their lovely little daughter. But the world isn't going to fall on her. Just learn to let go. You've taught her well, and she can only prove that to you and herself if you allow her to try out things for herself.

Be Actively Involved in Her Life

It is comparatively easier for dads to go for their son's baseball game on Saturday than it is to go for her stage play on Monday afternoon. That kind of stuff should be attended by stay-at-home moms, right? Well, not if you want to mean the world to your daughter.

As a single dad, you have more challenges than other parents. Coping with financial difficulties, too little time, your personal love life, and work schedule can all be very overwhelming! Kudos to you, but you still need to be there for your daughter as much as you can. You're all she's got, so you have to be actively involved in her life.

Teach Her about Boys and Dating

Boys! It is ironic how many dads (who obviously were once boys) try to protect their daughters from boys. *"Stay away from that good-for-nothing bloke! I can sniff his intentions from a thousand miles away!"* But you simply can't keep her away from boys for the rest of her life. Eventually, she'll have to stick to some bloke!

Instead of overprotecting her from boys and young men, teach her what she needs to know about boys and dating. Thankfully, chapters 7, 8, and 9 of this book give ample information about how to discuss puberty, boys, dating, sex, and the likes. I'll suggest you acquaint yourself with the information in those chapters.

In order to successfully guide your daughter through the phase of dating, you need to be honest and open with her. Tell her why you have reservations about her dating if you have any. Tell her why you are nervous if you are. Tell her the good, the bad, and the ugly aspects of dating. Be as balanced as you can so that she understands you are not merely trying to stop her from dating. Help her understand the role her hormones play on the feeling she has as a teenager. But most of all, make her see that dating is not merely about wearing the *"I have a boyfriend too"* badge. It is supposed to be the first step toward a lifetime commitment.

Bottom Line

Dear single dad, there may be a lot of things happening in your life right now that requires you to joggle between several aspects of your life. Nevertheless, the future of your lovely daughter depends largely on the guidance and protection you give her. No matter how busy you are, no matter how daunting the challenges you face, no matter the circumstances that resulted in your parental status, your daughter needs you. Do not fail her!

Chapter 7: Discussing Puberty with Your Daughter

Little Jane won't be a little girl forever. She'll eventually grow from that cute little bundle of joy to a girl who is mostly confused about the changes that are happening in her body unless someone tells her ahead of time what she should expect. That someone could be you, her friends, a doctor, or the internet. I'm guessing you'll prefer that that someone should be you because you are the only one who knows the exact views that are in consonance with the values of your home.

Many fathers tend to pretend not to be aware of the changes in their daughter. They shy away from talking about it, at least with their daughters. I mean, isn't it awkward enough that she's maturing into a woman? Why add to that the need to talk about it openly with her dad? But there is absolutely nothing awkward about puberty unless you choose to see it that way. Puberty is the most natural thing that will ever happen to any child. You didn't become an adult by skipping puberty; no one does! It is the natural order of things. So why should it be embarrassing to talk about it?

You run the risk of putting a mental and physical distance between you and your daughter if you avoid talking to her about the changes in her body. Moms do not usually have this problem because they have experienced firsthand what their daughter is going through. But dads are mostly guilty of this. Here's my advice to you as a dad or a male guardian—your daughter needs to hear from the strongest man she's ever known that she's still loved and beautiful in spite of whatever changes her body is going through. Mom can tell her that it's okay, but an encouragement coming from the opposite sex would make her feel more confident about herself.

First, you need to understand that puberty is simply the body's way of preparing the individual to be able to reproduce sexually. Long before any physical signs begin to show, there are several hormonal changes that occur internally that lead to physical change. If you get a good grasp of this understanding, then you can explain it to your daughter in simple and fun ways because it is nothing to be embarrassed about.

Also, keep in mind that puberty happens at different times for different children. So, do not be worried if your daughter is a bit early or a bit late compared to other girls. Don't go asking, *"Hey, Jane, why haven't you started growing boobs like your friend?"* That's an extreme example, but you get the gist, right? Don't fret and be all over her, checking her every now and then. There's no way she can skip puberty, so relax and let it happen naturally as it always does.

Dear Married Dad

Don't stay on the sidelines and watch your daughter from afar while she goes through one of the most important phases of her life. Be a part of this very crucial phase of her physical and mental development. But do remember to first discuss the issue with your wife to know how involved you should be. Should both of you contribute equally, or should your wife do most of the counseling while you offer moral support? Whatever you agree on is entirely up to both of you, but in any case, do not leave 100 percent of the talks and discussions to your wife only. No matter how limited your part is, play it well. Let your daughter know that your wife always keeps you in the know about her talks with her mom. And that it is all right if she needs more clarity or your view about it.

Dear Single Dad

You have some pretty tough job in your hands. If Mom is not readily available or you'll prefer not to involve her, then you may want to consider getting another woman involved. This is not to say you are shifting your responsibility to someone else. I'm suggesting this path because it is easier for your daughter to learn from someone who has firsthand experience about what she's going through. That experience, you may have read about or heard about but never really have. Puberty is quite different in males and females. Whatever knowledge you may have is purely theoretical. However, if no adult female can fit into the picture, then you will have to take it upon yourself to guide her through this phase. Remember that this is a very confusing period in her life. Don't let her search for meaning elsewhere; be there to give her all the meaning she seeks.

Dear Fathers

It doesn't matter if you are currently married, divorced, or a single father. Girls typically may not feel open to talk about their bodies with their dads, and that's okay. Do not force them into a discussion if they are not willing to. However, there are ways to make them open up and feel free to talk with you even about the most uncomfortable or awkward topics. Here are a few tips you may find really helpful.

1. **Gently introduce the topic**: "*Jane, today we are going to discuss vaginal discharge.*" What? For heaven's sake, you are not delivering a lecture! It is better to allow her to choose what she wants to talk about and then take it from there and gradually broach other related topics. Do not just dive headlong into discussing what your daughter may or may not be so keen to talk about. Start with something very mild like "*What do you think causes these funny-looking pimples on your face?*" "*Do you feel any physical discomfort?*"

2. **Include humor**: One of the reasons children dislike counseling is the serious attitude parents, teachers, and guardians have about it. Understand that you are dealing with your child who's just twelve or thereabout and not your colleague in the workplace. Replace the straight face with a warm smile. Interject your talks with jokes and funny talks. Make faces. Do crazy things that will get her to loosen up. Just make sure she gets it that you are not making fun of her but making the counseling process fun.

3. **Be her friend**: Do you know why your daughter

would rather talk about her body with her mom instead of you? Don't say it's because her mom is a female like her—no. Being a female like her is an added advantage and just by the way. The real reason is that her mom is her friend, not just a parent. If your daughter can find a true friend in you besides being her strong disciplinarian daddy, she'll pretty much become free with you as she is with her mom. This means, every now and then, you will have to get in touch with your inner child and let go of being her dad. Play with her. Spend quality time with her, talking about the things that are important to her. You cannot spend all your day focused on work, making money, and laying down house rules and expect that your daughter will warm up to you. Talk to her about the challenges you had while growing up. Tell her funny things she didn't know about you. Share quality laugher with each other, and in no time, she'll be as comfortable with you as she is with her friends and mom.

Puberty: What to Talk About

So, what exactly are you going to be talking about? I've compiled a list of some of the fundamental things you can discuss with her. Keep in mind to make it sound like your regular chat and not some therapy session.

Her Emotions

It is normal for girls going through puberty to have what can be described as an emotional roller coaster. She can easily lose grip on her emotions and begin to fuss or even cry over the most insignificant things. She may become over-reactive or oversensitive to things that ordinarily wouldn't matter. This is as a result of her body releasing waves of hormones that causes her mood to swing easily.

Make your daughter understand that these things are natural and will pass as soon as her body acclimates to the changes. Help her to see that it is no fault of hers and she shouldn't begin to think that there is something fundamentally wrong with her. Let her know that she is neither ill nor abnormal. Your goal should be to help her maintain the right perspective about these emotional spikes. This will help her cope with her changing body and feel less frustrated about being different than she was used to.

Her Feelings about Boys

Your daughter is going to have feelings for boys. Initially, boys may just be annoyances to her, but as she matures into puberty, she'll start feeling attracted to them. Make her understand that this is normal. It is nature taking its cause. And because it is the function of her hormones, she may not be able to stop herself from having crushes for boys. Let her understand that this is a normal phase in every girl's life and it will pass with time. Let her know that even though her sexual urges may feel very strong at this stage of her life, they will eventually wane and stabilize to a normal level as she grows older.

This is a time you need to guide her properly without coming on strong as being cagey or too strict and overprotective. She needs someone who will help her understand her feelings, not someone who will try to prevent her from experiencing those feelings.

Bodily Changes

During puberty, it is possible for some girls to begin to think and feel that they are ugly. They look at the mirror and see pimples or acne, probably one breast growing bigger than the other. Their vulva might appear very different, and hair might start to grow in all the unfamiliar places! It can feel both scary and confusing to your little girl. But that's why you are an adult who's had that same experience before.

Physical changes can also make your daughter insecure about her looks. This is especially true if she enters puberty a lot earlier or a bit later than most of her peers. She'll always feel like the odd one out when she's with her friends. This may make her become withdrawn to avoid the embarrassment of sticking out like a sore thumb. You need to constantly remind her that she is valuable, beautiful, and completely okay the way she is. There's probably a lot of emotional pressure she's going through because of her new looks, so you need to bring on your A game when it comes to reassuring her.

Periods and Virginal Discharges

For a father, perhaps the most awkward topics to talk about with your daughter are her period and virginal discharges. This, as well as the issue of sex, is a difficult topic to broach when dads talk with their young daughters. But these seemingly difficult issues shouldn't be left for the moms alone. Your perspective as a dad means a lot to your daughter.

But whether you are a dad or mom, you need to prepare your daughter's mind against her first period. Usually, breast development and pubic hair appearance precede the first menstrual period. This means parents have ample time to prepare their daughter's mind for her first period. Tell her what to expect, why it happens, and what she'll need to do to keep herself neat and tidy during the periods and other virginal discharges. Make her understand that her body is only getting ready to make her a beautiful mom. Tell her that her periods and virginal discharges are indications that she's a perfectly healthy and normal girl who will eventually have beautiful kids like her when she becomes a fully grown adult.

You may be lucky not to come from cultures where the menstrual flow is seen as a bad omen or dirty, but you may not be so lucky as to control whom your daughter interacts with. And if you do not give her the proper knowledge about these things, someone somewhere with a wrong notion may feed her some old wives' fables, and she'll buy into it and begin to see herself less than boys and men.

If you have a daughter who is already in puberty, she may be dying to ask a lot of questions about her menstrual period. Below are some questions she may have:

- What's the difference between a tampon and a pad?

- What happens if her period starts and she's not with tampons or pads?

- Can she go swimming during her period?

86

- What happens if the blood stains her pants or skirt?

There may be other things she'll want to know but may be too shy to ask you. You have to create an environment that encourages her to speak up and ask those nagging questions she's got. And for heaven's sake, if she does muster the courage to ask you anything about her period or bodily changes, do not react in a way that screams, *"I have no idea,"* *"This is embarrassing,"* *"Why are you asking me these kinds of stuff?"* or the ultimate no-no, *"I'm too busy to be bothered about you now!"*

Do not push her away by your reactions or your words. Instead, thank her for coming to you and confiding in you. Answer her questions to the best of your knowledge. If there is information you do not readily have, tell her you'll find out more and get back to her as soon as you can. If you are truly busy and cannot answer her questions immediately, briefly explain with a warm smile that her questions are in order. Let her know that you'll need a moment to clear up whatever urgent task you have at hand so that you can have all the time to answer her questions as well as talk about other related issues. Whatever you do, offer her encouragement to come directly to you with any questions she'll ever have.

Tell Her about Puberty in Boys

Your daughter may think that the changes she experiences are peculiar to girls only. Let her understand that boys also pass through that stage, and you can briefly explain how that happens for boys. This can be both enlightening and reassuring for her. She'll feel more confident of herself if she knows that all her peers, regardless of their gender, will, at one time, go through the same process she's currently going through.

Bottom Line

Make your daughter understand that she's not the only one going through the physical and emotional changes happening to her. Every other girl she knows is either going through or has gone through or will someday go through the same process. So, it's quite normal. Even if her entire face is covered with pimples and growth spurts and one of her breasts appears bigger than the other, assure her that she's as beautiful as ever and she's turning into a more beautiful and healthy woman.

Chapter 8: Let's Talk about Sex

How Close Are You to Your Daughter?

Have you ever wondered why your teenage girl feels totally embarrassed to talk about sexuality, sex, love, and other intimate issues with you but feels very comfortable discussing it with her peers or other adults? The reason is not farfetched: she doesn't think you'll understand her!

Why would a child you've raised from infancy think you wouldn't understand her? Simple: your attitude each time she brings up issues that are important to her tells her a lot about how you prioritize her views and feelings. As your daughter grows into a beautiful teenager, her mind keeps a record of her interactions with you. She will draw conclusions from the several interactions she's had with you in the past and determine if you are the right person to share her personal issues with. She will avoid you if you are always too busy to talk about her issues and if you are not always around when she needs to confide in you. Never shout her down when she airs her view, embarrass her each time she tells you something personal, or let her down when she confides in you.

If you find that your daughter isn't letting you in on issues relating to boys and her feelings and emotions, then it is high time you took a deeper look at how you have been relating with her. You need this personal review in order to be able to properly guide her from making serious mistakes that are capable of altering the course of her life. It is never too late to make amends if your relationship with your daughter is not too great. Remember, she is your daughter, and you have a whole more experience than her. So, you can tap into these vast experiences and gradually warm your way back into your heart. Then and only then can she open up to you and give you the opportunity to guide her aright.

Here are a few tips to draw her closer:

- Ask her on surprise dates. Make it special—just for the two of you.

- Spend quality time with her. It is not just the length of time you are with her but also the quality of the talk, play, and other stuff that you do with her that matters most.

- Develop special codes known only to the two of you. You can use that to communicate discretely when you don't want others around to know your intent. Your daughter will begin to see you not just as a parent but as a trusted friend too.

If You Think It's Uncomfortable, She'll Think the Same Too

Your daughter cannot feel free to talk about sex if you, as a parent, think it is an uncomfortable topic to discuss. It is an error to assume that *"she'll figure it out."* Your parents may have left you to figure it out by yourself, but you shouldn't repeat that same mistake.

Many parents and guardians will find the issue of sex very embarrassing to discuss, especially with their girl child, and that's because of the training they received. But that type of training doesn't help much; it only leaves the child to grope in darkness, trying desperately to find her way mostly through trial and error. What then is the purpose of being a parent? Why are you there to guide her? Of what value is your experience if you cannot guide your child through one of the most important decisions of her life?

It may be a big jump for you, especially if you are coming from a very conservative background, but you need to take the leap. If you do not know what to tell her, read books (like this one), do some researches, ask a counselor, or do whatever it takes to get over the uncomfortable feeling and broach the topic of sex with your daughter.

Don't tiptoe around the topic of sex as if it is a taboo to talk about it. Be at ease when talking about it, and she'll eventually become comfortable talking about it with you too. Lighten the air even if you choose to have a special time dedicated to this talk. Introducing humor will lighten whatever tension you both feel about the topic.

Always keep this in mind: if you shy away from talking to

your daughter about sex, you are the only one not telling her about it. Every other person (friends, media, internet) is telling her their opinions about it—opinions that may not tally with your home values.

The Approach

There are two major ways you can have this all-important talk with your daughter. However, keep in mind that the depth of discussion will depend largely on her age. Obviously, what you will tell a girl of about three to four years is completely different from what you will be discussing with your teenage girl.

Notice how I used the word "*tell*" as I referred to very little children and the word "*discussing*" when talking with a teenage girl. The reason is simple: at the tender age of three or thereabout, the child is merely inquisitive and simply wants to know without any intent to use the information immediately. So, you are basically telling or lecturing the child—feeding her information. However, with a teenager, you are not simply telling her about some information that may not be presently useful to her. That is why you will need to discuss—that is, share ideas—with her. She'll be sharing with you how she feels and what she thinks. In turn, you will be sharing with her your experience, pieces of advice, setting boundaries, and most importantly, giving her moral support.

Here are the two major ways you can approach this topic:

1. Setting aside time to discuss the issue and other uncomfortable topics

2. Seeking opportunities in your daily interactions to bring up the topic

The approach you choose depends on which method you think will get your daughter to participate fully and more comfortably. If she is the type that (1) likes to take notes, (2) can't cope with distractions, or (3) is matter-of-factly, then the first approach will work best for her. But if she is (1) very informal in her approach to learning, (2) likes to talk a lot, or (3) is very playful, then the second approach will work better for her.

Whatever approach you choose, make sure you do not simply lay down rules and think you have discussed with her. "*Don't do this or that*" or "*Don't think this or that*" doesn't usually work. As a matter of fact, it pushes your daughter far away from you with regard to discussing personal or difficult issues. Also, talking about sex is not a one-off event. So, don't just sit her down and have one lengthy discussion and then assume that the class is over! You've downloaded into her brain everything she needs to know about sex, so no more embarrassing talk about sex. That's not quite how it works. The discussion about sex has to be a running dialogue until she becomes an adult.

Here's a quick tip for breaking the ice when you notice that your teenage daughter is either too shy to discuss sex with you or can't fully express her thoughts. Ask her to write her questions on a paper and pass them to you. Alternatively, she can email or text you her questions. Some people are freer when writing than they are when expressing themselves verbally. However, you need to take gradual steps to help her graduate from only writing to speaking with you face-to-face.

At What Age Should You Start Talking to Her about Sex?

Realize that every child is at a different stage of maturity, so your discussion about sex has to be age appropriate.

Preschoolers (below Four Years Old)

Your little daughter of preschool age doesn't need to know the mechanics of sex. At that age, she is only wondering about a lot of "mysterious" happenings: Where did she come from? Why is Mom's belly protruding? Why are her parents' body features very different from hers?

At that age, they are not ashamed or embarrassed to ask anything, even in public places. Here are some nuggets of advice:

- Create an open atmosphere for discussing seemingly embarrassing topics. It doesn't matter how out-of-the-blue her question may appear to be. Be relaxed, calm, and straightforward about it.

- Do not frown at her for asking innocently. Please do not snap at her by saying things like, "*Where did you get that idea?*" Neither should you dodge her questions by changing the topic, saying, "*Go play with your friends, dear. They're waiting outside for you.*" Your daughter will get the message loud and clear: "I'm bad for thinking and asking such questions." Guess what? Next time, she'll save you the headache.

94

- Encourage her to ask more and be more open. Say things like, "*That's a brilliant question!*" And then go ahead and answer her question as simply as you can. Remember to end the little chat with something like, "*If you have any more question, please do ask me any time.*"

- Use the proper names for the body parts. Stop saying things like "wee-wee" or "pee-pee" when what you mean is vagina or penis. Don't start giving her the impression that using the proper names for body parts is embarrassing.

Always remember to keep things really simple at this stage. Do not give details that your daughter does not actually need. One way to know exactly how much information to give is to ask her what she thinks, and then you can expound more based on her level of knowledge. Don't go into a detailed explanation of how pregnancy results from sexual intercourse and then babies are born through the vagina of their mothers when what your daughter simply wants to know was where she came from.

If your little daughter is curious about where she came from, you can say something along the lines of "*You grew in Mommy's womb for nine months. When you were strong enough and ready, you were born.*" And please use "womb," not "tummy" or "belly." Food goes into the tummy; babies grow in the womb!

Elementary Years (Ages Five to Seven)

Teach your school-age daughter more about the biology of the human body.

- Tell her the difference between boys and girls.

- Explain the basics of pregnancy.

- Teach her about privacy. One way to do so is to knock before opening her door. She'll also remember to do the same when entering your room.

At this age, your daughter will be brimming with a lot of questions. Your answer to one question may lead to another question. Be patient with her and answer her questions. Be sure to prompt her for more questions using lines like, "*Is there something else you'd like to ask?*" or "*Does that make any sense to you?*"

Preteens (Ages Eight to Twelve)

This is a good time to start talking about the following:

- How to relate with boys

- The mechanics of sexual intercourse

- The biology of pregnancy

Teenagers

Your teenage daughter needs to be reassured that she can tell you anything. At this stage, it is very important to make her feel that you are her trusted ally. Although she's not yet an adult, you should see yourself as someone saddled with the task of preparing her for adulthood.

Talk to her about the following:

- Relationships, emotional connection, and lifetime commitments

- Physical intimacy

- Reproduction and how pregnancy can change her life completely

What Exactly Should You Talk About?

There is no one-size-fits-all when it comes to the exact message to communicate with your daughter. Family beliefs and values vary widely, and so are their views on sex and sexual behavior. Only you (the parents) get to decide under what circumstances you consider sex to be appropriate and moral. This means you get to choose how you want to raise your daughter with regard to sexual behaviors. You need to make your family values abundantly clear to her so that she knows what is expected of her.

It is okay to tell your daughter that you expect her to wait until she gets married to have sex if that is your belief. It is okay to tell her to say no to sex if you expect her to keep away from sex. Do not be afraid to set boundaries because you want her to be your friend.

Whatever message you choose to pass to her, be sure to be very open about it. Do not let the topic of sex to be hush-hush. Here's a quick checklist to know if you have adequately discussed the topic of sex with your daughter or you have simply brushed the surface.

1. Has your daughter had sex before? (Yes / No / I don't know)

2. Do you know if she has oral sex? (Yes / No / I don't know)

3. Have you had any discussion about STDs? (Yes / No / I don't know)

4. Have you told her how much physical intimacy is too much? (Yes / No / Not really)

5. Do you know if her friends have had sex? (Yes / No / I don't know)

6. If she's not had sex, have you asked her why? (Yes/No)

7. Have you told her your opinion on pre-marital sex? (Yes/No)

If your discussion on sex has not covered the above, then I'm afraid you've simply scratched the surface about sex talk. You need to dig deeper. Your motive for digging deeper should not be to find out if she's "guilty" but to offer proper guidance.

Dad or Mom: Who Should Do the Talking?

Both parents should talk to their child about sex. It is not uncommon for people to think that moms should talk to their daughters about sex while dads talk to their sons about sex. But you will be robbing your daughter of the perspective of her dad if only her mom does the talking. Mothers have a completely different perspective about sex than fathers do. Give your daughter the benefit of having both perspectives.

Equally, it is important to stress that both parents can have an open discussion with their daughter and, at the same time, talk to her individually.

Dear Dad

You were once a boy, and you definitely know how boys feel and think about sex and girls. You know that many boys see sex as a mark of becoming a man and that they are simply looking for a girl to prove how manly they've become. This is a false premise that, unfortunately, many boys believe. You can save your daughter a lot of emotional stress by sharing this perspective with her.

Make her understand that while she is innocently looking for a relationship, many boys are simply looking to conquer her. While she is longing for a romantic connection, many boys will take advantage of her innocence. Make her see that losing their virginity is more important to a lot of boys than finding romance.

Dear Mom

You were once a teenage girl, and most definitely, you know what many girls think about relationships and the undue pressure they get from their peers to become women.

Let your daughter know that it is okay not to want to have sex if she's not ready for it. Tell her that it is not proof of womanhood for a girl to have sex, as most girls have come to erroneously believe in recent times. Make her understand that sex is not a means for achieving some sort of social approval or power. She can still be a virgin and be as socially influential as any other girl.

On a General Note

Strict Rules versus Trust and Consequence

I do not mean to tell you how to run your family, but strict rules don't usually work with teenage girls. The stricter the rules, the more the likelihood of her violating them because she'll feel choked. No one likes being choked—especially teenagers. You need to loosen your grip a bit and let go, or else, she'll keep a lot of secrets away from you.

I'll suggest you emphasize trust and consequence. Show her that you trust her to keep to her agreement on family values, but if she breaks the trust, let her face the consequence that comes with that breach of trust. When you give her trust, you instill in her a sense of responsibility rather than a sense of being caged. So, when you are setting boundaries, do it in a way that includes her in the decision about what the boundaries are. In that case, the boundaries will become mutual agreements based on trust.

The key to making your child hold you in high regards, as well as trust you, is finding a balance between too much and too little discipline. If you come down hard on her each time she violates a rule, she'll cower in timidity. If you shut her away from you, you put a huge blockage in her path to developing her problem-solving capabilities. She'll always look up to you to make the decisions for her since she doesn't want to step out of the line in fear of your wrath. If you become too lackadaisical with her in the fear that you may push her away with too much strictness, she'll take you for a ride.

Take the middle path between obedience and freedom. It's similar to being a leader instead of a boss. Establish firm ground rules and be clear about what is expected of her without being bossy about it. Let your words and actions communicate your core family values, and she'll toe the line. You may not realize it, but you have a lot of influence on her.

What Are Your Expectations?

Many parents make the mistake of expecting the worst from their children, especially from teenagers. It is like there's almost an unwritten code that says, "Have all the fun with your kid while they are still very young because when they become teenagers, you'll be faced with the ordeal of coping with them."

Although this is completely ridiculous, parents still buy into that idea. That is why parents unconsciously pass the message that says, "You are only good if you don't engage in bad things, like having sex, doing drugs, and spending time with the wrong set of friends." Do not be surprised if these negative behaviors you dread so much begin to show up in your child. You expected it (unconsciously), so it's no big surprise if it happens.

I am not implying that these things are okay; I am only saying that, as a parent, you need to shift your attention away from focusing on the wrong things that your kid can get involved with and give your attention to your child's positive aspects—her hobbies and interest. It doesn't matter whether or not you understand or even like their hobbies and interests. Simply taking a genuine interest in their positive aspects can strengthen the bond between you and your child.

Early and Frequent Dating

Discourage early dating. It is a good practice to make your daughter understand that dating before she turns sixteen can get her into trouble that she's not ready for. If you make her understand this long before she asks if she can date someone, she'll know that you are not reacting to a particular individual when you say no to early dating.

When she eventually starts dating, make sure to limit the frequency with which she goes out on dates. You can encourage her to engage in group activities instead of one-on-one dates.

Discourage Dating Significantly Older Persons

For the safety of your daughter, make her see reasons why it is not in her best interest to date boys or young men who are by far older than she is. It is true that age difference does not really matter when it comes to matters of the heart, but for a teenager, it is important to set dating age limits even if it is an unpopular boundary. Set a limit of anywhere between two and four years age difference.

When your teenage girl is dating a significantly older boy, the physical strength difference, as well as the wide gap in experience and physical maturity, can lead to very risky situations that may place your daughter in harm's way.

Setting age limits can protect her from the following:

1. A forced sexual activity like rape, sexual assault, and sexual abuse

2. Taking undue advantage of her innocence and naivety

3. Emotional blackmail

4. Exposing her to sexual activities and contents (movies, porn) that may be repugnant to her

5. Unprotected sex and unplanned pregnancy

Giver Her Options That Are More Attractive Than Early Pregnancy and Parenthood

At an early age, help your daughter with her personal goal setting. Discuss her future plans—what career she'll to pursue. Help her break down her goals to daily, weekly, and monthly activities. Help her to understand that becoming pregnant as a teenager can truncate her dreams and goals. You are the parent with experience, so you have to make her see clearly what her priorities are. This is why I mentioned earlier that the job of parenting is not merely to provide and care for your child. It also involves you developing yourself to the point where you can also become a mentor to your child.

Let your daughter see that you value and cherish her educational pursuits. Do all in your power to keep her focused on her dreams and aspirations. Motivate her by providing access to books, her personal icons/models, and events that will inspire her to strive to become what she dreams of.

Take her academics serious. Be fully involved no matter how tight your work schedules are. Talk to her teachers if her grades are falling below expectation. One factor that can lead to teen pregnancy is poor academic performance. Failure in her academics can make her feel like a failure in life. This can spiral downward into giving up on her dreams and engaging in risky sexual behavior as a misguided way of releasing her frustration.

If she is engaged in after-school jobs, ensure that she doesn't spend too much time on the job. Let her have enough time for her studies, rest, and recreation. Also, try as much as you can to get her to use her spare time to engage in community service or some other constructive venture. Make her see that seeking ways to become a better person is far important than spending time thinking and doing things that can lead her into early parenthood.

The Effect of Separation and Divorce

The ideal situation for bringing up kids is in a home where both parents are happily married. They serve as living, breathing examples of what responsible parents should look like and how a happy home should be. Both male and female children will draw inspiration and emulate the behavior of both parents. The child needs the tenderness of the mother as well as the protection of the father. However, this ideal situation is not obtainable in every home. Life isn't always perfect in spite of our best intentions. So, if you are a parent who is currently divorced or separated or if you are considering those options, you need to factor in the effect it will have on your kids, especially the female child.

I do not mean to come across as being judgmental. However, you need to double your effort with regard to the proper upbringing of your kids. You will have to work more assiduously to maintain the connection you have with your kids, irrespective of who has custody. The fact that you are separating or divorced doesn't mean you cannot work with your ex as much as it is permissible to raise your kids properly.

Chapter 9: How to Discuss Sex with Your Teen

Know What to Say

Probably one of the main reasons many parents avoid the sex talk is that they do not know what to say. It will always feel awkward to talk about sex with your daughter if you are not prepared about what to tell her. Even when she asks questions, you'll either cleverly avoid her questions or fumble your way through it.

In order to be prepared, you need to do the following:

1. First, think about exactly what you would like to tell her. The more time you spend giving thought to what to say, the clearer you'll become.

2. Write down what you want to say. As you think about it, jot down your points so that you don't forget them. Whatever information you want to give her, whether it is about where to get birth control or how to practice safe sex, write it all down.

3. Next, practice the best way to present your talk. You can rehearse in front of your bedroom mirror or go over your notes with your spouse or friend. Actually, discussing the issue with your spouse will help to bring up more things to say to your daughter.

Present Facts, Not Only Personal Beliefs/Values

If all you did was to present her with a set of your own personal/family values and beliefs about sex without also laying bare the hard facts about sex, she might find out for herself what the facts are. If she finds out the facts from a source other than you, she'll have less faith in what you are telling her. *"Mom is just trying to live her life through me!"*

For the avoidance of doubt, tell her the facts and your personal or family values. Let her know the difference. For example, if your religious beliefs are against using birth control, make her understand that it is against your faith to do that but there is a science behind it. Then go ahead and explain the science to her. Whatever you do, don't just stop at telling her, *"It is a sin!"*

Tell her the difference between community beliefs (like the church) and scientific facts. For example, you can tell her that the church doesn't condone sex before marriage and you agree with the church. However, ask for her view and listen to what she has to say. Your goal is not to compel her to accept your views but to see the reason why your views are superior. If she understands your views, she can properly align them with science and accept them as hers too.

Talk about the Physical Aspects of Sex

Don't stop at being abstract. Be down-to-earth about the mechanics of sex. Use images on your laptop or from books to show her both the male and female reproductive organs and explain exactly how they work. Remember, she's a teenager, and you are preparing her for adulthood. It is not time to hide anything from her. Be as plain as can be.

Explain what pregnancy entails, exactly how it occurs, and what she'll go through. Talk about STDs (sexually transmitted diseases) and the dangers of having unprotected sex. Your goal should not be to scare her but to properly educate her.

Discuss the Emotional Aspects of Sex

Talk about how sex can increase the feelings she has for her sex partner. Let her understand that sex is not just a casual act; it is an intimate act that comes with a barrage of emotional entanglement. So, if she doesn't really like the boy or doesn't really know him, she shouldn't have sex with him. He may simply have sex with her and walk away for good, which will leave her heartbroken and may make her see all boys in the same light.

Let your discussion include talks about committed relationships. Teach her to look out for a boy who respects her and makes her feel really good about her personality. Ensure that you stress the need for mutual respect in a relationship that would lead to sex. Do not forget to explain to her the meaning of rape, sexual abuse, and sexual assault.

Listen Actively and Be Open-Minded

Remember, it should be a discussion, not a lecture. So, give room for her to talk and air her views or ask her questions. Keep away anything that may suggest to her that your attention is not fully with her. Don't look at your phone, the

TV, the magazine, or your laptop while she's talking. Give her your undivided attention.

When she says things that are not in accordance with your views, don't judge her and don't shout her down. You can say things like, *"I've never thought of it from that angle. What makes you think that way?"* You can also say, *"I'm not judging you in any way. I'm simply trying to understand what you are getting at."*

She'll Ask Questions: Be Prepared

There is no telling how your daughter will respond or react. Nevertheless, be prepared for a barrage of questions if she is the inquisitive and outspoken type. And even if she is the reserved type, she may have a couple of very sensitive questions that will require some serious thought before answering. In any case, if you do not know the answer to any of her questions, you can simply tell her that you'll be glad to help her find out the answer. Make sure you do so promptly and give her an honest answer.

Here are some questions your daughter may ask:

1. How do I know that I'm ready to start having sex?

There is no rush when it comes to sex. Having a beautiful relationship built on mutual trust, respect, and genuine care is far more important than rushing into sex. There are many other ways to get intimate without having sexual intercourse. Having sexual arousals doesn't necessarily mean you have to act on those impulses. Focus first on being in the right relationship, and you'll know when the time is right for sex.

2. Is oral sex the same as sexual intercourse?

Technically, no. You can't get pregnant through oral sex, but you can get STDs from oral sex.

3. What? His what goes into my what?

Umm, well, that's the idea. It sounds very awkward now because you are a teen. With time, you'll fall in love with him being inside you.

4. Does it hurt?

It depends on the girl. Many girls feel pain, especially the first time or the first few times. Some other girls don't feel any pain. Being nervous about sex can prevent the vagina from being lubricated, which can cause an uncomfortable experience. This is why you need to use a lubricated condom. It lubricates the vagina and provides protection against unplanned pregnancy and STDs.

5. Is it true that sex is really fun?

Sharing the most intimate moments of your life with someone you trust is fun. However, if there is no mutual trust and respect, you may regret sharing those precious moments with someone who simply took you for granted. That is why there is no need to rush into a relationship and sex. Take your time to know the person you want to share your special moments with.

6. What if I don't like sex at all?

There is absolutely nothing wrong with you if you don't have interest in sex at all. Some girls do feel that way initially. However, as you grow older, your body will

*naturally want it, and you'll gradually start to develop
an interest in it.*

7.   Are you saying you and Mom [you and Dad] have sex
     every night?

*No, not every night. We love each other dearly, and we
express our love for each other every day, but sex is not
the only way to express love.*

8.   I've been dating him for three months now. Is it too
     early to have sex?

     *There is no specific time for dating before sex. The
     important thing to keep in mind is not how long you
     have been dating but how comfortable you are with
     the idea of having sex. It is possible and normal to
     date someone for years without having sex.*

9.   My boyfriend is pressuring me to have sex. Should I
     say yes?

*You should have sex when you are ready. No one, not
your boyfriend, not your peers, should pressure you to
do what you don't want. If he insists on sex, then he
doesn't really care about you.*

10. I've told him no, but why does he think I'm just
     pretending?

*Saying no to him must go beyond your words to your
body language, as well as the way you dress when you
go on a date with him. You cannot be saying no with
your words but you dress or perhaps your body
language is screaming yes. He is a boy, and boys are
more visually stimulated than girls. So, watch what you
show him when you are with him.*

11. I've had sex before. Can I still say no to sex?

You can always say no to sex. You are young and beautiful, and sex shouldn't be your primary concern for now. But it doesn't matter if you've had sex before. You are not broken.

12. Can I have a French kiss?

Understand that boys naturally have a higher sex drive than girls. It is not his fault or making; he is built that way to ensure the continuity of the human species. Prolonged kissing, French kiss, and fondling may be your way of showing affection; but it may lead a boy to be very sexually aroused and increase his chances of pressuring you for sex. So, if you are not ready for sex, do not tempt him with sexual behaviors that can result in sexual intercourse. Set your boundaries with him. If he truly cares about you, he will respect those boundaries.

13. Is masturbation wrong?

Pleasuring yourself using masturbation is not so much a matter of right or wrong. Rather, it is a matter of whether or not you can control the behavior and the effects it can have on your relationship. Masturbation is very likely to turn into an addiction. When it does, it may likely cause some very negative effects on your sexual behavior toward your partner. The most logical way to avoid such negative effects is not to engage in masturbation, to begin with.

14. What is wrong with pornography?

The focus is not on building healthy relationships but purely on sex. Porn can make you want to try things out that may hurt you emotionally. Besides, pleasure in porn is mostly faked; it doesn't happen that way in real life. Porn can give you distorted perceptions and false expectations about sex that will leave you dissatisfied in real life.

I have attempted to prove basic answers that may or may not be in line with your family values and personal beliefs. Ultimately, the response or answers you give to your daughter should be in keeping with what you believe to be true and the type of woman you'll want your daughter to become.

Be Honest

There's no point lying or twisting the truth in order to make her do what you want. She may ask if you waited until you were married before you had sex. Be truthful in your response. If you waited, say so without embellishing the story. If you didn't wait, simply say you didn't but you wish you did wait. The truth and your honesty will increase the level of regard and respect she has for you.

Also, do not scare her by trying to blow things out of proportion. Do not tell her she could catch an STD by flirting with boys or some other outrageous lie. Remember that your goal is to keep her safe as much as you can. Being dishonest about sex talks can make her distrust you if and when she finds out, and she eventually will.

Be Firm, Be Affectionate

It is a balancing act when dealing with your teenage daughter. Show her that you love and adore her and will always support her no matter what. But let her know that you are firm about your family values. Don't have double standards about boundaries; neither should you let her have her way because you love her too much.

Be open-minded but don't let her take you for granted. Do not be afraid to implement rules that the family has agreed upon. For example, if there are curfews, ensure that she and every other person observe it. If you do not want her to be alone at home with her boyfriend, make sure she obeys the rule.

If your daughter is already having sex, do not be afraid to ask her what birth control method she is using. It is your right as a parent to know so that you can properly offer her guidance.

Remember to Follow Up

As mentioned in the previous chapter, talking about sex with your daughter is not a one-time event. You need to let her know that she can come to you any time if she needs to know more or talk more on the issue. Be sure that you keep the lines of communication open at all times. Let her know that situations are bound to change so that she can approach you anytime there's a new development.

Equally, you need to be proactive and follow up on your previous talk. Do not just sit and hope that she'll come back for more talks. This is not likely to happen if she is not very comfortable with the talk the first time. You need to gently push for more. After a few days of the initial talk, you could go to her and say something along the lines of *"You did great the last time. Thank you for being open. Would there be anything else you'd like to know more about? Have you thought of any new thing that you'd like me to explain?"*

Questions to Make Her Think

If you would prefer that your teenage daughter waits until she gets married or at least until she's a fully grown adult before she has sex, you can use the following questions to drive home your message. Your goal should be to get her to think about the questions and not just to elicit an immediate answer from her. I'll suggest that you drop the questions within your conversations one at a time. Cleverly weave them into your chitchats so that it doesn't sound as if she's under interrogation.

1. Do you think girls should wait for marriage before sex?

2. Do you think teenage girls who have sex planned for it or it happened by accident?

3. What do you think increases a girl's chances of unplanned sex?

4. What do you think will happen to you if you got pregnant by mistake?

5. Can you think of some emotional risks associated with sex before marriage?

6. Are there physical risks of sex before marriage?

7. Are you planning on waiting or experimenting?

8. What is your best friend planning on doing: waiting or experimenting?

9. Would you feel good if your future husband has had sex several times with several other girls?

10. Is there actually safe sex?

Even if you do not have any preference with regard to her waiting or not waiting for marriage before sex, this line of questions will prompt her to give serious thought to the issue of sex. She'll not take sex lightly like girls who have no proper guidance do.

Bottom Line

The uncomfortable feeling and awkwardness about discussing sex with your teenage girl will gradually diminish the more you practice talking with her. It is a learning process for both you and her, so do not fear that you will make a mistake and say something you are not supposed to say. There is always room for making corrections. If you find out after your talk that you have given her wrong information, you can go back as soon as you discover the error and apologize for your mistake, and then give her the correct information. That way, your daughter will have more trust and confidence in you and understand that infallibility is not a human trait. She'll live her life without being afraid of making mistakes and without being under any pressure to be perfect.

Chapter 10: Don't Do This . . . Ever!

In this final chapter, I shall highlight a few things you should never do as a parent or guardian if you must raise your girl child to become a confident and purpose-driven member of the society.

Don't Quit Your Job

Dear mother, as a parent, you love your kids and will do anything for them. You have the tendency to see yourself as 100 percent responsible for your children. This often puts you in a position of sacrificing yourself for their happiness. But whatever you do, do not quit your day job so that you become a stay-at-home mom. Don't you ever do that!

As a mother, becoming a full-time caregiver may look like the commendable thing to do, and I would have agreed with that view if we were still living in the nineteenth century, but we're not. The times have changed, and believe it or not, humans have evolved in the last few decades. I would like to suggest that you give up any thought of quitting your day job for the sake of your kids, especially if you have a daughter or female children. The reasons are quite simple and straightforward.

1. **You cannot be a working role model to your daughters**: A study conducted by Harvard Business School has shown that daughters of working mothers earned 23 percent more than those whose mothers stayed at home (*New York Times*, 2015). The study, which sampled 50,000 adults from across twenty-four countries, showed that there was growing evidence that indicated that daughters of working mothers are more likely to put in more years of education, gain employment, and earn more wages than daughters of stay-at-home moms.

   It is natural for a mother to feel the need to spend more time with her kids, and that is very helpful for the children too. However, there is a need to find a balance between constantly spending time with them and staying away from them for very long periods of time. Working is a strong message to your children (especially the girls) that they need to fend for themselves. Boys, when they become adults, naturally do understand that they need to work in order to fend for themselves and their families. Girls, on the other hand, will most likely grow up to believe that they need someone to care for them, fend for them, and protect them if they grow up in a home that has a stay-at-home mom. A mother can change her daughter's perception of being self-reliant if she is a working mom.

2. **You are sending the wrong message to your sons**: If you happen to have male children, you are training them to see women as suitable for housekeeping only. You do not have to say a word from your mouth before they get the message. When

they grow up with a stay-at-home mom, they'll think that is the norm. The effect this has on them may not show up until they go into relationships and start saying things like, *"What do you need the job for? I can provide for you and the kids!"* or, *"My mom raised us without a nanny, and there were four of us!"*

A woman who wants to work has more chances of doing so if she marries a man whose mother worked (*The Quarterly Journal of Economics*, 2004). So, if you want your daughter to be a working mom or to get married to a man who will support her ambition to work, do your best to be a living example to her.

3. **You set yourself up for frustration**: Giving up your job for the sake of raising your children can rob you of the joys in your moments and can leave you frustrated in the end. What happens when you spend your entire life giving up your joy and happiness for the sake of your kids and they turn out to do the exact opposite of what you have always feared? You watch all your years of sacrifice go up in one puff of smoke. Frustration and resentment take over you. Resentment is anger turned inward. Since you do not want to vent the anger on your beloved kids, the only person to lash out against is yourself. This path can lead down to depression, and that certainly is not good for you.

It's okay if you are a stay-at-home mom. It's okay if you work from home. What is not okay is to quit your job because you want to provide, protect, and be there for your daughter. Your child needs you as a guide, not as someone who controls her. Trying to be 100 percent present with her all the time is another form of control. You are unconsciously seeking to have an input in every single thing she does. You are depriving her of the ability to use and develop her intuition, instincts, and intelligence.

If your current situation makes you stay at home, use that opportunity to show your little girl what great things moms can do even when they do not go out for a job. Let her watch and join you as you happily do the chores. Do not give her the impression that you are a full-time caregiver because you have no other choice. Let her see that it is a noble thing to take care of the home and the family. Let her see that the happiness of a home depends largely on great moms like you, and that's who she'll become one day. Make her understand the importance of working as a woman and a mother and teach her that she doesn't have to sit and wait idly for anyone to cater to her. She can be useful whether she is at work or at home.

Don't Turn Down Practical Skills Because You Are Female

The notion that some skills are the exclusive domain of men is very ancient! Do not let gender define what skills you should or should not have. While it is okay to let the man perform so-called manly tasks, there is nothing wrong for a woman to do these tasks also. Your daughter who is always looking up to you as a role model may be very interested in learning hands-on practical skills. Do not discourage her by your attitude toward so-called unladylike skills. Little Jane won't want to get her hands all dirty if her mom raises her nose at practical skills.

Don't Apologize When You've Done Nothing Wrong

It seems like the normal thing to do in order to "let peace reign," right? Wrong! Some parents (mostly mothers) are so used to saying "I'm sorry" even when they're clearly not at fault. It's like the hallmark of submissiveness and humility, but in truth, it sends a very wrong message to the person you are apologizing to. It tells them that you consider yourself less than them; it says clearly that you have a problem with self-worth. When you apologize for no reason, you are saying you deserve far less than the person you are apologizing to. But all that does not compare to the wrong message you are sending to your daughter. You are effectively telling your little daughter, "*Women are wrong by default and are worth far less than others!*" Now, that's a completely false premise to feed into your little daughter's mind.

Also, saying sorry to your child when you have not done anything wrong tells her that she can manipulate you at will. Don't give your daughter the impression that she's right 100 percent of the time. It is quite well to be gentle, but do not forget to be firm also.

Don't Ever Say This to Her

"*Stop being bossy!*" That phrase has the capacity to drastically erode a girl's confidence. The sad part is that this phrase is thrown around little girls without recourse to the effect it has on their psyche. When your daughter behaves in a manner that you consider rude, resist the temptation to shout her down with "*Stop being bossy!*" Simply state what she's doing that you do not like.

It's ironic how adults find suitable words to say to boys even when they are rude but are at a loss for the right words to use when it is the girl child who is being rude. Boys are encouraged when they assert themselves. Adults see an outspoken boy as a natural leader, but an outspoken girl is told not to be bossy. This sends a clear message to the girl child: "You are to be seen, not heard!" The effect? The girl child eventually develops less interest in leadership roles after being told to "*stop being bossy*" many times. To her, society doesn't support the idea of females being in charge.

Have you noticed how less frequent girls are given airtime to speak or answer questions in class? If that is not easily noticeable, you would have noticed that girls are frequently interrupted in class than boys. What message do you think that attitude sends to the girl child? Does it say, "*We want more of your gender in leadership positions*," or does it scream, "*You're unfit to lead*"?

It is alarming to note that between elementary and high school, a girl's self-esteem drops about 3.5 times more than that of a boy. The girl child is held back from assuming leadership roles because she does not want to be seen as bossy.

If you truly want to build her confidence, do your daughter some good and ban the word "bossy" from your home! Let your little girl know that there is nothing wrong in females taking the lead role. When the girl child grows up in an environment that encourages her natural ability to lead, she'll have no fear about standing up for herself, her ideas, and others too.

Ask around and you'll hear people, both men and women, wishing more women were in leadership positions in politics, business, technology, and even in the corporate world. It is not enough to want more women in power. Steps must be taken to make sure that happens. Women do not become women all of a sudden. No, they grow from little pretty fragile girls into women. It is the program we drum into them that they carry forward into womanhood. So, if you discourage your little girl at home by calling her bossy, guess what? She'll most likely not be interested in stepping into the shoes of a boss.

Don't Let Her Witness Conflict without a Resolution

Whatever you do, spare your daughter the trauma of witnessing a major argument or conflict with your spouse or another adult. They don't need to see their parents in such disagreeable light. However, since it may not always be possible to completely shield them from all forms of disagreements, take it upon yourself to allow her to witness how you resolved the issue if she has witnessed the conflict.

As a mother, when your daughter sees you in an argument with her father, try as much as you can to make her see also how you two worked out a compromise. If that is not feasible, explain to her, after the resolution, how both of you were sorry and apologized to each other. Doing this tells your daughter that, although you are her perfect role model, you can be wrong sometimes and that it is okay to say sorry when she is wrong.

When you make her understand that it is okay to admit that you are wrong when you are at fault, you are, in effect, teaching her how a responsible woman should behave during a conflict. Keeping her away from this knowledge is setting her up for some serious issues with conflict resolution as she matures into adulthood.

Don't Encourage Beauty over Brains

Little girls are so adorable! You'll have to have stones for a heart not to want to compliment their pretty cuteness in their dainty little dresses. *"You look so cute and beautiful in that princess gown!"* It helps to build their self-esteem, right? Well, that may not be totally correct.

If the first thing everyone tells a little girl is how cute her dress is or how pretty she looks, we are telling her that we value her looks over her brain. Pretty soon, that little girl will start spending more time in front of the mirror. She'll start worrying about her weight at a very young age and start considering dieting even when her body needs all the food it can get to produce enough growth hormones. When she becomes a young teenager, she'll start thinking of breast implants and cosmetic surgery.

This may sound like an exaggeration, but it isn't. In her book *Think: Straight Talk for Women to Stay Smart in a Dumbed-Down World*, Lisa Bloom, an attorney and bestselling author, revealed some shocking statistics. She says that 15–18 percent of girls wear lipsticks, eyeliners, and mascara regularly and they are just under the age of twelve! Also, 25 percent of young American ladies do not care much about winning the Noble Peace Prize; they would prefer to be America's Next Top Model. In 2009, a study from the University of Central Florida showed that nearly half of all three- to six-year-old girls are seriously concerned about their body weight (ABC News Network, 2011).

The question is "Are they just being naturally self-conscious, or are we training them to be so?" Beginning from the home, the girl child is made to believe that her appearance is more important than the content of her brain. We have created a culture that first focuses on the girl's appearance before any other thing. This puts the girl under constant pressure to appear ever pleasing and hot. Have you noticed the slim sexy women on the cover of magazines? With such images constantly in front of our daughters, what do you expect they assume of our societal values with respect to their body shape? This path only leads to unhappiness because the girl child is led away from her true self to a self that must appear sexy and attractive to society. Her thoughts, ideas, and accomplishments are pushed to the background; and her sexiness is brought to the fore.

Avoid this path by encouraging the girl child to engage in intelligent discussions. Depending on the age of the girl, talk about books, ideas, concepts, and her likes and dislikes. Allow her to express her ideas freely and do all you can to diminish any talk about clothes, hair, makeup, and the likes. Let her see that you are more interested in the value of the ideas she holds in her brain than her physical appearance.

Also, ensure that you are not making comments that suggest that you are always trying to improve her appearance. If she's comfortable appearing like a tomboy, do not force her into being like a princess. Let her know her options and allow her to make her choice.

It is important to also recognize that there are several body types. If your daughter is within a healthy weight range, please do not suggest, in any way, that she cuts back on what she eats. Telling her about what she eats is indirectly telling her that she is not good enough as she is. Such a girl is likely to fuss and worry about her body and may begin to diet too early in her life due to a nagging sense of not being good enough.

Don't Talk Bad about Your Body

Your daughter is listening! The way you feel and talk about your body affects how she sees hers. If you are constantly making negative comments about your body parts, guess what? Your daughter is going to pick that up and start seeing her body in that negative light. She is simply mirroring you! Unfortunately, this can negatively affect her confidence level about her body as there is the likelihood of passing your negative judgment to her body too.

You need to be the strong, positive-minded, and body-confident adult she looks up to. Don't ever pass a message that says you feel less than gorgeous! No matter how imperfect you think you are, your kids look up to you as their hero and heroine. Be a good example to them and say nice things about yourself, especially when they are around. Mean it when you say those nice things; your children can easily spot it when you are telling a lie! They are that smart.

It is okay to be honest when you do not like something about your body. If it is something you can correct, such as your weight, make your daughter understand that you are working to make that thing right. But if it is something you cannot do anything about, stop complaining about it and accept your body the way it is.

It is a grave mistake to compare yourself to other women in a way that puts you down! Another woman's accomplishments may indeed be greater than yours, but it serves no good use if you put yourself down because of that. Instead, use those accomplishments to motivate your daughter. Let her see that there is no limit to what she can accomplish if she sets her mind to it.

Comparing yourself to another woman's appearance, especially what you see in the media, is another mistake. Those images in the media are very unrealistic. Make it your duty to de-emphasis appearances; looks are really unimportant and shouldn't form a basis for comparison at all.

One thing to also keep in mind as a mother is to never cancel an outing based on the excuse that you do not have something pretty to wear. Doing that is telling your daughter that socializing is all about her appearance (how hot she looks) and never about the experience of enjoying the company of the people you are going to meet. That's completely backward! Socializing is not about showing off, so don't pass that message to your naive daughter.

Don't Talk Bad about Her Appearance

In as much as you shouldn't pass on to her a negative self-image of yourself, do not also engage in name-calling or making defaming remarks about your daughter's body. Although she is still a child, it can negatively affect her self-esteem.

Whatever you do, do not embarrass your daughter by showing her not-so-pleasant photographs to others! Do not humiliate or shame your daughter in front of her peers. Don't make fun of her before others. These things can linger in her mind for a lifetime and can cause her to become timid in some aspects of her life.

Do not use the word "fat" when describing your daughter. That word has a very negative effect on her and how she sees herself. If you have a daughter that is outgrowing her dresses, let her know that it is normal for humans to outgrow their clothes, especially when they are young. And for heaven's sake, never say, *"You're too big for that dress."* Instead, say, *"That dress is small for you."* The idea is to not pass a message that makes it sound as if she is getting too fat or too big. If she is worried about her dress size, tell her that sizes on clothes depend on the brand and manufacturer. A mom can show her daughter several of her dresses with different dress sizes from different brands to ease the daughter's worry about her dress size.

Don't Flirt to Get Special Treatment

You've violated traffic rules while driving little Jane back home from school. To wriggle your way out of a ticket, you begin to flirt with the officer, and he lets you go. What you forgot was that little Jane was watching you closely all the while and learning faster than you could ever imagine! What did she learn? Little Jane learned an important lesson from her mom that day: the value of a female lies in her sexuality and appearance! It will take a lot of time, effort, and some serious explanation to undo that lesson.

Dear mother, even if you are given to flirting and being a stripper, kindly restrain yourself when your kids (especially your daughters) are present. The damage your action will cause may be irreparable for a very long time. Stop being a stripper in the presence of little Jane unless you want her to come home pregnant when she's just sixteen!

Dear father, do not bribe your way out of an offense, especially when your child is watching. That's the worst kind of message to pass to your impressionable child. Equally, do not bribe your child to behave well. A bribe is not an effective tool to use in teaching your child responsibility and respect.

Don't Disrespect or Undermine the Other Parent

There are no perfect relationships. Adults love themselves and their troubles, but please spare your kids the drama. Do not involve them or get them to take sides. Whether you are having a mild disagreement or you are currently separated or even divorced, do not use that as an occasion to badmouth the other parent in the presence of your child. The child has a right to experience the love of the other parent.

If you are a mother who is currently not in good terms with your husband, talking bad about your husband in the presence of your daughter sets her up for future difficulty in trusting the men that'll come into her life. If you must say something not cool about her father, make sure that is not anywhere close by.

Don't Emphasize Her Inadequacies

What you focus upon expands. If you always point out your daughter's shortcomings and weaknesses, your awareness will always pick out her flaws because that is what you are giving your attention to. She'll become a source of unhappiness to you.

On her part, she'll become less confident about her abilities and grow up to feel that she is deficient in some way.

As much as it lies in your power, avoid negative criticism on her academic performance. Saying things like "*You are such a failure*" or "*You are a disappointment*" can cause immediate demoralization and future damage to your child's self-esteem. Remember that failure is an event, not a person. She may have performed poorly in her academics, but that doesn't make her a failure.

If your daughter has performed poorly in her subjects, appreciate her for her efforts in other subjects or other areas where she has performed well even if it has nothing to do with academics. After that, encourage her to put in more efforts in improving in the areas where she has challenges.

Being point-blank, direct, or brutally forthright with your kids, especially your daughter, when their performance falls below your expectation can cause severe damages that may take several years to fix. Direct bluntness shows a brazen lack of tact. You should apply the "shit sandwich" method of feedback used in the workplace to communicate your child's shortcomings. You've not heard of the shit sandwich? Well, that's one more homework for you!

And while we are on the subject of pointing out your daughter's inadequacies, let me quickly add that children do not understand sarcasm. Being sarcastic at your child at the slightest misbehavior only leaves the child more confused and unhappy. The same thing goes for shouting at them in anger. You can correct a child without necessarily shouting at them in anger. When you point out the wrongdoing or behavior, they get the message. Shouting does the exact opposite of what you intend it to. Instead of instilling correction, it instills fear and self-doubt and causes your child to be sad.

Shouting at kids is one habit many parents find difficult to let go of. *"Jane can be so annoying. She drives me out of my skin!"* Yes, I know. That's why you are an adult and she's a child. You must develop, through consistent practice, the need to remain calm always, especially when communicating with your kids. This is why the process of being a true parent or guardian is the same as the process of personal development.

Don't Compare Her to Anyone

Comparing your daughter to any other child puts undue pressure on her. You are telling her to quit being herself and be like another person, whether she has the capability of the other person or not. While it is good to expect high performance from your kids, holding them to the standard of another person is really unfair.

Encourage your daughter to be unapologetically her authentic self. There is nothing wrong with not being the best in one subject or some other physical activity. As long as she is comfortable about putting in her best in whatever she does, that is good enough.

Don't Tell a Lie in Front of Her

All parents lie. That's a given. You have lied to your kids and to other people. It may be a harmless white lie, but it's still a lie. While you may not be able to completely avoid lying (I mean, we are humans, right?), you shouldn't do it in front of your daughter (and son too!). Lying in front of your daughter is setting a wrong example for her. How would you possibly succeed in teaching her not to lie to you or to other people when she sees you doing it so well?

Don't Gossip about Other Women

Bringing down other women seems to be a trendy topic when women meet. Don't engage in badmouthing or speaking poorly of other women or other people in general, especially if your daughter is present. Let her see you as someone who supports, encourages, motivates, and inspires other women to become better people. This will go a long way to help her establish long-lasting friendships with other girls who centers on building each other up instead of tearing each other down in mindless competitions.

Don't Watch Trash TV Shows

Fighting and vulgarity seems to be the central theme of some of the reality TV shows nowadays. For example, those that focus on wives, the so-called *Real Housewives* of this or that. Curse words are freely thrown around, and fights can start off for the most nonsensical reason. That is not the type of TV show you would want your daughter to watch. It has nothing useful to offer that innocent daughter of yours. While it is not humanly possible to shield your little innocent girl child from real-life violence, it is absolutely unnecessary to expose her to such crude and mindless interactions.

Don't Spend Too Much Time on Gadgets

Children learn faster by observing those around them. You are their parents and the closest example they spend most of their time with, so they will naturally emulate what they see you do. If your daughter is forming the habit of spending most of her day watching TV or chatting online on her phone or laptop, she probably saw you doing the same thing.

When you spend too much time in front of the TV or with your gadgets, it can make your daughter think you value those things more than how you value her, or she may think that's the proper way to spend most of her time.

Develop the habit of playing with your daughter outdoors rather than wasting away precious time constantly in front of the TV. Read good books, and you'll be silently encouraging her to toe the line.

Bottom Line

How would one ever cope with all these don'ts? Wouldn't this keep the parent or guardian in a continuous cautious mode? Well, it doesn't have to be so. When you have practiced being responsible enough times, it comes to you naturally. You do not have to be one person when your child is not around and then magically transform into a responsible parent when your child emerges from her bedroom.

While you are trying to be responsible, do not give your child the impression that her presence is obstructing your conversations or interactions. Children can read these subtle messages, so be sure to be free with them and show them that they are welcome to be with you at all times.

Living a life of double standards is not the goal of positive parenting. You simply have to become a better father or mother in order to raise better children.

Conclusion

How does it feel reading all the dos and don'ts? Overwhelming, right? But that's not my goal. Remember that there is no such thing as a perfect parent or guardian. If you paid close attention while reading through this book, you would have discovered that one of the goals of this book is personal development. It seems very unlikely to use a book on how to raise a girl child to teach personal development. However, the truth is that you cannot even begin to come close to raising a child (boy or girl) if you do not possess an ample dose of maturity—not maturity in the sense of your age but maturity in what it takes to be a model, coach, and mentor, because that is what you are to your child.

Take all the time you need to study this book. You may not be able to follow all the ideas presented here 100 percent of the time (no one really does!), but you have to make a commitment to give it your best for your sake and for the sake of your child.

You may have to make some adjustment in your lifestyle as you get set to implement what you have learned in this book. It is okay to falter and fail sometimes. You are human, and that is expected. Your daughter may get on your nerves, and you just lose it. It's perfectly okay. Just remember to explain to her that you are working on making your relationship better. Make her understand that you may make mistakes sometimes but that doesn't mean you love her less.

If you have a girl child who's already coming into puberty or is a teenager and with whom you've not had a pleasant relationship up till now, it may be a bit awkward to begin to warm your way back to her. But keep in mind that she is your daughter. No matter how things have turned out in the past, you can make a fresh start and begin to make things better. Be open about your learning process and get her involved. She'll work with you if she sees your honesty and sincerity of purpose (just don't start by imposing dos and don'ts on her!).

Human behavior does not change automatically. It is a gradual and continuous process. Your little girl may behave in ways that you do not like now. Do not assume that telling her what to do once will transform her life once and for all. There is no switch in her that you can simply turn on and off to make her behave as you wish. You need to be patient with her. Realize also that this book was not written with the goal of making your daughter do as you wish. Instead, I have written this book with the intention to help you raise and nurture your little princess into her authentic self. Release the need to mold her into an image that suits you. Provide her with several opportunities that will make her choose what truly suits her.

Best wishes for everything!

References

ABC News Network. (2011). *Body image issues: 6-year-old girl worries she is fat*. Retrieved from https://abcnews.go.com/US/body-image-issues-year-girl-worries-fat/story?id=13880833

Bloom, L. (2011). *How to talk to little girls*. Retrieved from https://www.huffpost.com/entry/how-to-talk-to-little-gir_b_882510

Curtin, M. (2016). *Want your daughter to succeed? Ban this word in your house*. Retrieved from https://www.inc.com/melanie-curtin/want-your-daughter-to-succeed-ban-this-word-in-your-house.html

Edwards, J. (2016). *10 things you just shouldn't do in front of your kids*. Retrieved from https://www.shefinds.com/10-things-you-just-shouldnt-do-in-front-of-your-kids/

Kashef, Z. (2017). *How to talk to your preschooler about violent events in the news*. Retrieved from https://www.babycenter.com/0_how-to-talk-to-your-preschooler-about-violent-events-in-the_3657112.bc

New York Times. (2015). *Mounting evidence of advantages for children of working mothers*. Retrieved from https://www.nytimes.com/2015/05/17/upshot/mounting-evidence-of-some-advantages-for-children-of-working-mothers.html

The Quarterly Journal of Economics. (2004). *Mothers and sons: Preference formation and female labor force dynamics.* Volume 119, issue 4, pp. 1249–1299. Retrieved from https://academic.oup.com/qje/article-abstract/119/4/1249/1851071

Woolston, C. (2017). *10 tips for raising a confident girl.* Retrieved from https://www.babycenter.com/0_10-tips-for-raising-a-confident-girl_10310248.bc

Woolston, C. (2017). *Gender identity: What shapes boys and girls.* Retrieved from https://www.babycenter.com/0_gender-identity-what-shapes-boys-and-girls_10310676.bc

The Journal of Clinical Endocrinology & Metabolism (2018). *Behavioral interventions to prevent childhood obesity: A systematic review and meta-analysis of randomized trials.* Retrieved from https://academic.oup.com/jcem/article/93/12/4606/2627263

US National Library of Medicine (2004). *Prevalence of overweight and obesity among US children, adolescents, and adults, 1999-2002.* Retrieved from https://www.ncbi.nlm.nih.gov/pubmed/15199035

Made in the
USA
Middletown, DE